Christian Martyrdom

Christian Martyrdom

A Brief History with Reflections for Today

EDWARD L. SMITHER

CASCADE *Books* · Eugene, Oregon

CHRISTIAN MARTYRDOM
A Brief History with Reflections for Today

Copyright © 2020 Edward L. Smither. All rights reserved. Except for brief quotations in critical publications or reviews, no part of this book may be reproduced in any manner without prior written permission from the publisher. Write: Permissions, Wipf and Stock Publishers, 199 W. 8th Ave., Suite 3, Eugene, OR 97401.

Cascade Books
An Imprint of Wipf and Stock Publishers
199 W. 8th Ave., Suite 3
Eugene, OR 97401

www.wipfandstock.com

PAPERBACK ISBN: 978-1-7252-5381-0
HARDCOVER ISBN: 978-1-7252-5382-7
EBOOK ISBN: 978-1-7252-5383-4

Cataloguing-in-Publication data:

Names: Smither, Edward L., author.

Title: Christian martyrdom : a brief history with reflections for today / Edward L. Smither.

Description: Eugene, OR: Cascade Books, 2020 | Includes bibliographical references and index.

Identifiers: ISBN 978-1-7252-5381-0 (paperback) | ISBN 978-1-7252-5382-7 (hardcover) | ISBN 978-1-7252-5383-4 (ebook)

Subjects: LCSH: Martyrdom—Christianity—History | Martyrdom—Christianity | Persecution—History | Christian martyrs

Classification: BR1601.3 S665 2020 (paperback) | BR1601.3 (ebook)

Manufactured in the U.S.A.   02/26/20

"For our brothers and sisters in Christ who are persecuted for their faith"

(BOOK OF COMMON PRAYER, 2019, 128)

Contents

Acknowledgements | ix
Abbreviations | x
Introduction | xi

1 We Worship a Suffering Servant | 1

2 The Christian Life Is about Suffering | 10

3 In Martyrdom We Witness | 30

4 In Martyrdom We Are Prophets | 42

5 In Martyrdom We Worship | 57

6 Reflections on Martyrdom for the Twenty-First-Century Church | 68

Bibliography | 73
Index | 79

Acknowledgements

Since this work grew out of classroom discussions, I wish to thank my history of global Christianity and history of mission students at Columbia International University who allowed me a venue to think out loud about the place of martyrdom and suffering in the Christian story. I also want to acknowledge my CIU leadership who allow writing and reflection to be built into my job description.

I am thankful for my friend Todd who suggested that I write a book on Christian martyrdom. I am eternally grateful to Ruth, my beta editor and writing coach, who read this entire manuscript and made many helpful recommendations.

I am indebted to my wife Shawn for her love, support, and patience in the writing process.

Finally, I am grateful for friendships with suffering believers, especially North African friends, who have taught me unwavering faith and resilience.

Abbreviations

ANF Ante-Nicene Fathers
CSB   Christian Standard Bible
KJV   King James Bible
NPNF Nicene Post Nicene Fathers
NIV   New International Version

Introduction

It's amazing how quickly things changed. On April 18, 2007, two Turkish pastors, Necati Ayden and Uğur Yuksel, and a German missionary, Tilmann Geske, welcomed five Turkish young men to an evangelistic Bible study. The pastors ran a Christian publishing house and led a small church in the southeastern Turkish city of Malatya. Posing as seekers with questions about the gospel, the five young men were actually part of a radical Islamic group. Once the Bible study began, they tied the pastors up, tortured them, and then slit their throats. They filmed the entire affair.

News of the brutal massacre quickly spread throughout Turkey through the news media. Not only were many Turkish Muslims horrified by the murders, but they were also shocked by the response of the men's widows. When asked to comment about the events and the men who killed their husbands, the women declared that they chose to *forgive* them. Their message—a powerful witness for Christ—was also transmitted by the press all over Turkey.

As the legal process for the five men dragged out for nearly a decade and justice was slow in coming, the Turkish church reflected on its identity as a minority faith movement in a Muslim country. Not long after the murders, one Turkish pastor remarked: "While we do face hardship, I would not necessarily call the Turkish church the persecuted church. And yet with this event it suddenly was the persecuted church."[1]

---

1. "Malatya," https://www.youtube.com/watch?v=4mSEeSZbejQ (accessed

Because of their deaths, Necati Ayden, Uğur Yuksel, Tilmann Geske, their families, and the Turkish church suddenly had a witness for Christ that they did not have before. The Turkish church calls them the Malatya martyrs. They take their place in a line that stretches down through history. In this book, we will meet martyrs, reflect on their lives in light of Scripture, and consider the place of suffering in the Christian faith.

Confusion about Martyrdom

Before going further, we should address a few common questions and objections about martyrdom. *First, doesn't martyrdom exist in other religions and ideologies, and is it therefore not unique to Christianity?* Indeed, since the rise of Islam in the early seventh century, Muslims have celebrated martyrs *(shuhud)*, especially those who died defending Islam during a holy war *(jihad)*. In recent years, some Muslim suicide bombers have also been remembered as martyrs. An increasing number of Tibetan Buddhist monks have also set themselves on fire and become martyrs, protesting China's political oppression of Tibet. Finally, during World War II, Japanese *kamikaze* pilots gained fame for crashing into Allied targets, including planes and ships. Though not religiously motivated, these pilots became martyrs for the Japanese military cause.[2] So many religious and political movements have a place for martyrdom, with some elements that actually compare well to Christian martyrdom. While the focus of this book will be on martyrdom within Christianity, I will not argue that dying for one's faith (Christianity, Islam, Buddhism) makes that belief system true.[3]

Second, aren't martyr stories merely Christian inventions that exaggerate Christian suffering? Isn't the aim to create a martyr consciousness among groups like North American evangelicals to

---

May 27, 2019). See further James Wright, *Martyrs of Malatya*.

2. See further Middleton, *Martyrdom*, 1–5.

3. Christian apologist Josh McDowell (*More than a Carpenter*, 56–68) makes this argument for the Christian faith in his chapter on martyrdom, "Who would die for a lie?"

encourage a movement of culture warriors? This is Candida Moss' argument in her book *The Myth of Persecution* (2013). Scholars of the early church agree with Moss that the first three centuries of Christianity were not filled with non-stop persecution against Christians. On the other hand, the consensus of scholarship accepts the fact that Christians did face discrimination and, at times, persecution in the Roman Empire prior to the rise of the Emperor Constantine. This opposition was uneven and inconsistent, but this certainly does not erase real instances of discrimination, oppression, and even violence. Even after Constantine brought peace to the church in the Roman Empire in the early fourth century, Christians continued to suffer under the Zoroastrian kings in neighboring Persia.

Moss' additional claim that an imagined early church persecution has fed a martyr complex among groups like American Christians today remains an uncompelling argument. Any group can develop a victim complex. However, it is difficult to correlate that to the history of a movement such as the church. In this book, our commitment is to discuss accounts of Christian martyrdom—both ancient and modern—based on reliable historical accounts.

Finally, haven't there been excessive and exaggerated emphases on martyrdom in church history? To be sure, during the Emperor Decius' mid-third-century oppression of the church in the Roman Empire, martyrs—those who stood firm in their faith, went to prison, and even died for their faith—were accorded a special priestly status by some believers. This was particularly the case in North Africa. Bishop Cyprian of Carthage (195–258) challenged these excesses and sought to clarify a proper view of church leadership and spiritual authority. Later, some North African believers who had denied their faith by making sacrifices to the Roman emperors sought to rehabilitate themselves spiritually by seeking martyrdom. In the fourth and fifth century, some members of the Donatist church also pursued voluntary martyrdom. Confronting this poor understanding of grace and the gospel, Augustine of Hippo (354–430) argued that committing suicide did not make one a martyr.[4] While such excessive views and practices have certainly persisted through church history, this book will not deal with those who sought martyrdom to earn salvation or a higher spiritual status.

Defining Martyrdom

Given these misunderstandings and objections, for our purposes, martyrdom simply refers to those who witness unto Christ through laying down their lives. They are killed because of their faith in Christ.

From Scripture, the word martyr (*martys*) literally means "a witness." The verbal form (*martyreō*) captures the action of witnessing. In much of the New Testament, martyrs refer to those who were eye-witnesses of Christ. However, in Revelation 2:13, John adds further meaning by using martyr to describe those who witnessed unto Christ by giving their lives. Everett Ferguson adds that this is how the word was commonly used by the church by the end of the second century.[5] Amid the most intense periods of persecution during the first three centuries of the church, many were executed for refusing to offer incense or sacrifices to the pagan gods or emperors. In short, throughout church history, many believers have witnessed through their words, by enduring suffering and persecution, and through giving up their lives for the gospel.

Martyrdom is the extreme end of a wide spectrum of persecution and must be understood in that context. Thus, in addition to martyrs, at times I will discuss those who demonstrated a willingness to face martyrdom, those who suffered hardship and persecution and even expected death, though they did not actually die for their faith. They, like the martyrs, bore witness for the gospel and have much to teach the western church today.

---

4. See further see Fox, *Pagans and Christians*, 442–60; Frend, *Martyrdom and Persecution*, 254–84, and Ferguson, "Martyr, Martyrdom," 726–27.

5. See further Ferguson, "Martyr, Martyrdom," 724.

Introduction

Literature

Despite Moss' claim that early church persecution is a Christian invention, any survey text of early Christianity must deal with the status of Christians in the Roman Empire, discrimination against the church, and periods of deliberate persecution, both localized and occasionally empire-wide.

A number of authors have written specific works on persecution and martyrdom in church history. W. H. C. Frend's *Martyrdom and Persecution in the Early Church* (first published in 1965) is a classic work on suffering in early Christianity. Showing the influences of the book of Daniel and the Jewish Maccabean revolt, Frend presents the church as a suffering movement within the Roman Empire. In an introductory work, *Martyrdom: A Guide for the Perplexed* (2011), New Testament scholar Paul Middleton compares the notion of martyrdom in Christianity, Judaism, and Islam. In the first half of the book, the author looks at a history and theology of Christian martyrdom, which is very informative for our current project. In her scholarly monograph, *Ancient Christian Martyrdom* (2012), Candida Moss takes a fresh look at martyrdom by focusing on the first two centuries of the church and examining the reliability of martyr texts. She argues that diverse perspectives and theologies of martyrdom developed. In her popular book *The Myth of Persecution* (2013) Moss goes considerably further by claiming that early church persecution is a later Christian invention. Despite this revisionist approach, any study of the issue in early Christianity will have to deal with the status of Christians in the Roman Empire, discrimination against the church, and clear periods of deliberate persecution. Moss' theory that early martyr stories are a fourth-century invention has received strong push-back from other scholars working in the field, and while some of her observations and arguments have merit, her overall case remains wanting. This book hold to the majority view that periodic persecution and martyrdom were a stark reality for the early church.

Focusing on suffering in the twentieth-century global church, Paul Marshall authored *Their Blood Cries Out: The Growing Worldwide Persecution of Christians* (1997). In a follow-up work with Lela Gilbert and Nena Shea, Marshall wrote *Persecuted: The Global Assault on Christians* (2013). In both books, which are written on a more popular level, Marshall aims to raise awareness of the suffering global church in order to call the church in the West to prayer and advocacy.

These works, a mix of scholarly early church sources and more accessible modern studies, will greatly inform the present work. My focus will be admittedly simpler.

Aim of this Book

In this book, I explore suffering, persecution, and martyrdom as formative aspects in the story of Christianity. In an effort to make sense of suffering as an expected and even welcomed aspect of the Christian life, I will discuss this theme biblically, theologically, and historically.

The thread of suffering weaves through the history of Christianity. The earliest followers of Christ worshipped a Suffering Servant. Many of these first-century believers also suffered, even laying down their lives for their faith. Though many nations have accorded Christians religious freedom and even privilege, suffering and martyrdom continue to be a reality for many in the twenty-first-century global church.

Beginning with the life of Jesus (chapter 1) and the testimony of the early church (chapter 2), in these pages I explore the reality of Christian martyrdom through Christian history and with biblical reflection. We will meet martyrs, tell their stories, and show that through martyrdom we identify with Jesus and pursue a faith that does not shirk from suffering. Through suffering and martyrdom, we witness unto Christ (chapter 3), raise a prophetic voice against the kingdoms of this world (chapter 4), and worship the living God (chapter 5). By encountering these lives, readers are challenged to identify with those who suffer in the twenty-first century and to cultivate a place for suffering in their own Christian experience (chapter 6). Though most global Christians will not die for their faith, a theology of Christian martyrdom will aid believers to identify more closely with Christ and to embrace suffering as a normal part of the Christian life.

I

We Worship a Suffering Servant

He was despised and rejected by mankind, a man of suffering, and familiar with pain. Like one from whom people hide their faces he was despised, and we held him in low esteem. Surely he took up our pain and bore our suffering, yet we considered him punished by God, stricken by him, and afflicted. But he was pierced for our transgressions, he was crushed for our iniquities; the punishment that brought us peace was on him, and by his wounds we are healed. We all, like sheep, have gone astray, each of us has turned to our own way; and the Lord has laid on him the iniquity of us all. He was oppressed and afflicted, yet he did not open his mouth; he was led like a lamb to the slaughter, and as a sheep before its shearers is silent, so he did not open his mouth. By oppression and judgment he was taken away. Yet who of his generation protested? For he was cut off from the land of the living; for the transgression of my people he was punished. He was assigned a grave with the wicked, and with the rich in his death, though he had done no violence, nor was any deceit in his mouth. Yet it was the Lord's will to crush him and cause him to suffer, and though the Lord makes his life an offering for sin, he will

see his offspring and prolong his days, and the will of the
Lord will prosper in his hand. (Isa 53:3–10)[1]

This is how the Prophet Isaiah described his famous Suffering Servant.[2] Because the Servant endured God's wrath, took the punishment for sinners, physically suffered without any verbal defense, was put to death and buried, and then resurrected, most post-Easter Christians reading Isaiah understood the Suffering Servant to be Jesus the Messiah.

Through direct quotes or allusions to Isaiah 53, the Gospel writers overwhelmingly conclude that the Suffering Servant was Christ (see Matt 8:17; 27:57–60; Luke 22:37). During Phillip's encounter with the Ethiopian eunuch in Samaria, in which Phillip unpacks the meaning of Isaiah 53, Luke notes: "Then Philip began with that very passage of Scripture and told him the good news about Jesus" (Acts 8:35). In his letter to dispersed believers dealing with hardship, Peter exhorted the church to imitate the example and sufferings of Christ and "follow in his steps" (1 Pet 2:21). He then describes the character of Jesus by quoting a portion of the Suffering Servant passage (Isa 53:9, 5, 6).

Jesus also affirms that Isaiah was talking about him. In one instance, Jesus quotes directly from Isaiah 53 to describe his ministry of suffering (Luke 22:37; Isa 53:12). In Mark's Gospel, Jesus announces his purpose for his life and ministry, one that involved suffering and parallels Isaiah's description: "For even the Son of Man did not come to be served, but to serve, and to give his life as a ransom for many" (Mark 10:45).

Through his incarnation, life, earthly ministry, and passion, suffering framed the life of Jesus. In this chapter, we explore Christ's suffering at each of these points to show that Christian martyrdom and suffering is first founded on the basis that we worship a Suffering Servant.

---

1. Unless otherwise noted, all English Bible references are the New International Version (NIV).

2. See further Isa 40–55.

Suffering in the Life of Christ

Humiliation in the Incarnation

Jesus' suffering began in his incarnation—when the eternal Son of God took on flesh (John 1:14). He was humiliated in becoming the God-man. In what was probably a hymn sung by the first-century church, Paul admonishes the earliest Christians to pursue humility by following the example of Christ:

> Who, being in very nature God, did not consider equality with God something to be used to his own advantage; rather, he made himself nothing by taking the very nature of a servant, being made in human likeness. And being found in appearance as a man, he humbled himself by becoming obedient to death—even death on a cross! (Phil 2:6–8)

Though the cross was the pinnacle of Christ's suffering, in the incarnation Jesus denied his divine privileges, "made himself of no reputation" (Phil 2:7, KJV), became as a servant, and lived with the limitations and pain of being human. Jesus' life on earth began in a posture of suffering and serving.

A Refugee

Following the visit of the gentile kings from the East who came to worship the Messiah (Matt 2:1–12), the Jewish King Herod, fearful of losing his throne, began a systematic program of eliminating his future political opponents by putting to death all male children under the age of two (Matt 2:16–18). Before the killing began, Matthew records:

> An angel of the Lord appeared to Joseph in a dream. "Get up," he said, "take the child and his mother and escape to Egypt. Stay there until I tell you, for Herod is going to search for the child to kill him." So he got up, took the child and his mother during the night and left for Egypt, where he stayed until the death of Herod. (Matt 2:13–15)

Because of their forced displacement due to political tyranny and genocide, Joseph's family fits the modern definition of a refugee. Jesus of Nazareth was a refugee. In the Lord's displacement, he identified with sojourners, strangers, and the wandering Israelites in the Old Testament as well as the suffering diaspora church in the New Testament. He also identifies with people on the move who have sought refuge through the centuries, including those in the present day.

A Poor, Working Family

Following Jesus' birth, Mary and Joseph presented him at the temple and offered "a sacrifice in keeping with what is said in the Law of the Lord: 'a pair of doves or two young pigeons'" (Luke 2:24). According to the Law (Lev 12:8), a family ought to offer a sheep, but if they lacked the financial means, then doves or pigeons were also acceptable. The offering for Jesus was a poor family's sacrifice.

Though Jesus apprenticed as a rabbi and certainly gained skills in reading and interpreting Scripture, he also apprenticed with his earthly father Joseph in the building industry. He worked with his hands and arrived home many days dirty and with bodyaches, scrapes, and splinters. After Joseph's death, Jesus' family was put in a more vulnerable economic state, but the Lord continued to provide for his widowed mother and family through his work as a builder.

The Gospel writers, particularly Luke, emphasized Jesus' ministry to the poor. Jesus was well trained for this work because his family background and humble vocation allowed him to identify with the poor.

Suffering in His Call to Ministry

Each of the Synoptic Gospel writers capture the striking event of Jesus' baptism (Matt 3:13–16; Mark 1:9–11; Luke 3:21–22). While identifying with humanity in his baptism by John the Baptist, Jesus also invites the presence and power of the Godhead to the baptismal waters. The Spirit descends in the form of a dove as the Father verbally communicates his pleasure with the Son.

In what seems like an instant, the jubilant celebration turns to hardship. Using his customary economy of words, Mark bluntly writes: "Immediately, the Spirit drove him into the wilderness" (Mark 1:12, CSB). The same Holy Spirit who descended at Jesus' baptism (and who shared fellowship with the eternal Son since eternity past) forced Jesus into the wilderness for forty days of testing. This period paralleled Israel's forty years (Deut 9:18) and Elijah's forty days in the wilderness (1 Kgs 19:8). Weak from fasting, Jesus is approached by Satan on three different occasions. Satan tempts the Lord to turn stones into bread (to satisfy his physical hunger); to throw himself off the top of the temple (doubting God's ability to care for him); and to bow do Satan in exchange for earthly kingdoms (power). To each temptation, the Lord responds with memorized Scripture from Deuteronomy and stands firm until the devil leaves and angels come to care for him (Matt 4:1–11; Mark 1:12–13; Luke 4:1–13). Jesus' ministry was inaugurated by two events—his baptism and forty days in the wilderness. His three-year public ministry was launched in physical hardship and spiritual temptation.

Hardship in His Earthly Ministry

Hardship, pain, disappointment, and rejection shaped much of Christ's earthly ministry. Leaving his work as a builder to become a full-time preacher and disciple-maker, Jesus embraced voluntary poverty and lived an austere lifestyle. To maintain his ministry, he was dependent on the hospitality and material support of others.

After the initial period of testing in the wilderness, Jesus' itinerant ministry continued to include encounters with demons and spirits. This spiritual warfare ministry, along with preaching and caring for the crowds, did take a physical toll. Because of this, Luke notes that Jesus "often withdrew to lonely places and prayed" (Luke 5:16)—a strategy for refueling from the fatigue of ministry.

Jesus also experienced the hardship of opposition on a number of levels. Matthew, Mark, and Luke each record how the residents of Nazareth rejected him (Matt 13:53–58; Mark 6:1–6; Luke 4:16–30). To this rejection, he famously responded, "A prophet is not without honor except in his own town, among his relatives and in his own home" (Mark 6:4). In Luke's account, the Nazarenes took issue with his Sabbath-day claims of being the Messiah and reacted with violence: "All the people in the synagogue were furious. . . . They got up, drove him out of the town, and took him to the brow of the hill on which the town was built, in order to throw him off the cliff" (Luke 4:28–29). In all of the Gospel accounts, Jesus' hometown ministry was limited because of disbelief.

The Gospel writers also show that the Jewish leaders regularly opposed Jesus' ministry and teaching. They reacted negatively to his habit of table fellowship with sinners and tax collectors as well as his ministry of healing on the Sabbath (Mark 2:15–16; Luke 7:36–50). They also sought to trap him with questions about his teaching and authority (Matt 22:15–45).

The Passion of Christ

In reading the four Gospels, the evangelists seemingly hurry through the life and earthly ministry of Christ in order to get their readers to the foot of the cross. John dedicates almost half his Gospel to the final week of Christ's life, while Mark devotes about forty percent of his. While the biblical narrative climaxes at the cross, Jesus experienced various types of physical and emotional pain during the entire passion week.

After the triumphal entry into Jerusalem on Sunday, Jesus wept over Jerusalem on Monday. His grief stemmed from the people's spiritual blindness and the city's impending destruction (Luke 19:41–44). Later that day, he confronted the money changers and salesmen in the temple, cleansing the temple from their exploitation and reminding everyone present that God's house "will be called a house of prayer for all the nations" (Mark 11:17; Matt 21:12–17). On Tuesday, Judas, one of the Twelve, begins to conspire with the Sanhedrin to trap Jesus and hand him over in exchange for money.

After a silent Wednesday, Jesus sits down at table on Thursday to celebrate the Passover with his disciples. During the meal, Jesus demonstrates further incarnational humility by washing his disciples' feet (John 13:1-20). He illustrates the service *(diakonia)* that characterized his earthly ministry and what he was calling his disciples to do. Around the table, he predicts the betrayal of two disciples—Judas and Peter. Finally, at this Upper Room meal, Jesus inaugurates the Lord's Supper—a meal that would forever celebrate his broken body, shed blood, and finished work at the cross (Matt 26:17-30; Mark 14:12-31; Luke 22:1-23).

After supper, Judas decamps to implement his plan of betrayal, while Jesus heads to the garden of Gethsemane with his disciples to pray. He asks that they keep watch and pray, but they fall asleep. Though Judas greeted the Lord with a kiss—a gesture of hospitality—he used it to point out Jesus to the Jewish leaders so they could arrest him (Matt 26:36-56; Mark 14:32-52; Luke 22:39-53).

Between midnight Thursday and daybreak Friday, the Sanhedrin convenes three trials. Though finding Jesus guilty of blasphemy, the Sanhedrin lacks the political authority to convict Jesus so they send him to Pontius Pilate (fourth trial) who quickly sends him to Herod (fifth trial). Herod sends Christ back to Pilate (sixth trial), who has him beaten and turned over to be crucified (Matt 26:57-68; 27:1-2, 11-31; Mark 14:53-72; 15:1-20; Luke 22:63-71; 23:1-25). Forced to carry his own cross most of the way to Golgotha, Jesus is nailed to it and experiences a Roman execution by crucifixion. Around three o'clock on Friday, Jesus "gave up his spirit" (Matt 27:50) and died.

Taken off the cross and placed in the borrowed tomb of Joseph of Arimathea, the Lord spends Holy Saturday in the grave. On the third day, Mary Magdalene and the other Mary arrive at the empty tomb and encounter the risen Lord (Matt 28:1-10). Later, he appears to the rest of his disciples.

Christian Martyrdom

To proclaim the gospel—the good news of our Lord Jesus Christ—is to declare his suffering. In one of Paul's simple gospel presentations, he declares: "Christ died for our sins according to the Scriptures, that he was buried, that he was raised on the third day according to the Scriptures" (1 Cor 15:3-4). As the early church leaders prepared believers for baptism, they focused their teaching on the basics of what a Christian ought to believe. This teaching, initially expressed in third- and fourth-century baptismal creeds, became crystallized in the early seventh-century declaration known as "The Apostle's Creed":

> I believe in Jesus Christ, his only Son, our Lord.
> He was conceived by the power of the Holy Spirit
> and born of the Virgin Mary.
> He suffered under Pontius Pilate,
> was crucified, died, and was buried.
> He descended to the dead.
> On the third day he rose again.
> He ascended into heaven,
> and is seated at the right hand of the Father.
> He will come again to judge the living and the dead.[3]

Most of these affirmations about the life and redemptive work of Christ have to do with hardship, pain, and suffering. About the manner in which Christ died, Christopher Wright asserts that "the cross was the unavoidable cost of God's mission."[4] Hans Boersma adds that the Father allowed the Son to experience violence through the cross in order to extend his divine hospitality to sinners.[5] Scott Sunquist summarizes: "Jesus is the suffering love of God for the world, Jesus is the salvation of God."[6]

---

3. "The Apostles Creed," http://anglicansonline.org/basics/apostles.html (accessed June 3, 2019).

4. Christopher Wright, *The Mission of God*, 312.

5. See Boersma, *Violence, Hospitality, and the Cross*, 14–16.

6. Sunquist, *Understanding Christian Mission*, 199.

Summary

Suffering frames the incarnation, life, and redemptive work of Christ. The gospel of Jesus Christ is good news because of Christ's suffering. To construct a Christian faith without the work of Christ—especially his crucifixion, burial, and resurrection—is to deny historic Christian teaching.

To follow Christ also means to embrace hardship, suffering, and even persecution. Before the cross and during Christ's earthly ministry, Jesus called his disciples to suffer: "Whoever wants to be my disciple must deny themselves and take up their cross and follow me. For whoever wants to save their life will lose it, but whoever loses their life for me will find it" (Matt 16:24–25; also Luke 14:27). As believers participate in God's kingdom mission—between the *now* and the *not yet* of the kingdom—suffering becomes normal. In a sermon on suffering and God's redemptive plan, Bishop Gregory the Great (540–604) stated:

> The Father sent his Son, appointing him to become a human person for the redemption of the human race. He willed him to come into the world to suffer—and yet he loved his Son whom he sent to suffer. The Lord is sending his chosen apostles into the world, not to the world's joys but to suffer as he himself was sent. Therefore, as the Son is loved by the Father and yet is sent to suffer, so also the disciples are loved by the Lord, who nevertheless sends them into the world to suffer.[7]

Believers through the ages have identified with Jesus by embracing hardship. Christians are motivated to suffer and even welcome martyrdom because of their love for Christ—because they worship a Suffering Servant.

---

7. Gregory the Great, *Forty Gospel Homilies,* 26, cited in Crosby, *Ancient Christian Devotional,* Kindle Locations 967–70.

2

The Christian Life Is about Suffering

Martyrdom is extraordinary, but it is not unique. Jesus of Nazareth, ten of the twelve disciples, and the apostle Paul all died as martyrs. Their testimonies shaped the early Christian community, setting the tone for an expectation and embrace of suffering. Commenting on the motif of suffering in the New Testament Scriptures, Scott Sunquist asserts: "The authors of the New Testament were apostles (sent ones) and martyrs (witnesses), reflecting on the meaning of the missionary of God (Jesus) even as they were sharing in his sufferings."[1]

To further establish the biblical basis for Christian martyrdom, in this chapter we argue that suffering is a prominent theme in and element of the Christian experience. To support this, we examine the suffering journey of the New Testament church, the early church in the Roman Empire, the rise of monasticism, as well as other suffering voices from church and mission history.

---

1. Sunquist, *Understanding Christian Mission*, 199–200.

The Suffering New Testament Church

Just prior to his ascension, the Lord promised the apostles: "You will receive power when the Holy Spirit comes on you; and you will be my witnesses in Jerusalem, and in all Judea and Samaria, and to the ends of the earth" (Acts 1:8). While Luke makes "Jerusalem to ends of the earth" his outline for Acts, he also depicts suffering and hardship as the catalysts that propel the church on mission to the nations. Irvin and Sunquist note: "the earliest Christian missionaries from Jerusalem went out as refugees and victims of persecution, . . . these first Christians had expansionist tendencies without worldly power."[2] To show this, we discuss how the early apostles, Paul, and the first-century church experienced suffering while serving in mission.[3]

Jerusalem and Judea

Throughout Acts, the apostles' ministry combined power—healing, miracles, and supernatural acts—with gospel proclamation. While ministering around Solomon's Portico (Acts 3–4), Peter and John heal a lame beggar and then preach the gospel to a captive audience. As a result, they are quickly dragged before the Jewish Sanhedrin, which was "greatly disturbed because the apostles were . . . proclaiming in Jesus the resurrection of the dead" (Acts 4:2). The Jewish leaders ordered the apostles to stop their activities and then released them.

Returning to Solomon's Portico for more healing and preaching (Acts 5:17–41), the apostles were arrested by the high priest and thrown into prison. During the night an angel opened the prison doors and instructed them to go back to the temple courts and continue their ministry. When brought back before the Sanhedrin and ordered to explain their actions, the apostles asserted, "We must obey God rather than human beings!" (Acts 5:29). Furious

---

2. Irvin and Sunquist, *History of the World Christian Movement*, 26.
3. See further Schnabel, "The Persecution of Christians in the First Century," 525–47.

with the apostles, the Sanhedrin planned to execute them until the influential Jewish leader Gamaliel intervened. Stymied, the Jewish leaders had them flogged and then released them.

In Acts 6, we meet Stephen, "a man full of faith and of the Holy Spirit" (Acts 6:5), who was among those chosen to wait on tables and care for the Greek and Hebrew widows of the Jerusalem church. In addition to this service, Stephen was a persuasive preacher who performed signs and wonders. Opposed by Greek-speaking Jews in Jerusalem, Stephen was brought before the Sanhedrin where he delivered an extended gospel presentation, including a thorough recap of Israel's history. The Jewish leaders responded by dragging him outside the city and stoning him to death. Stephen became the first recorded martyr in the Jerusalem church (Acts 6:8—7:60).

Present at Stephen's stoning, Saul of Tarsus became an agent of persecution against the church during this period. Luke writes: "On that day a great persecution broke out against the church in Jerusalem, and all except the apostles were scattered throughout Judea and Samaria" (Acts 8:1). Other believers scattered to Tyre, Sidon, Cyprus, and Antioch, among other places.[4] The church at Antioch of Syria was planted as a direct result of the upheaval in Jerusalem and because of the witness of believers from Cyprus and Cyrene in Antioch. Describing the launch of this multi-cultural church, Luke continues:

> News of this reached the church in Jerusalem, and they sent Barnabas to Antioch. When he arrived and saw what the grace of God had done, he was glad and encouraged them all to remain true to the Lord with all their hearts. He was a good man, full of the Holy Spirit and faith, and a great number of people were brought to the Lord. (Acts 11:19–24)

While caring for this church, Barnabas invited Paul, the persecutor-turned-Christian missionary, to labor with him in Antioch. Barnabas probably recruited Paul because of his diverse background,

---

4. See further Schnabel, "The Persecution of Christians in the First Century," 527–28.

training, and previous experience in cross-cultural ministry (Acts 11:25).[5]

Meanwhile back in Jerusalem, King Herod arrests James, the brother of John, and puts him to death by the sword (Acts 12:1–24). Desiring to win favor with the Jews, Herod tosses Peter in prison ahead of an intended trial. For a second time, Peter is miraculously led out of prison and rejoins a house church that was praying for him. In an interesting turn of events, Herod is struck down by an angel and eaten by worms for refusing to honor God.

Paul's Missionary Work

After his dramatic conversion on the road to Damascus (Acts 9:1–19), Paul became a Christian evangelist. He encountered much suffered and hardship. Paul likely didn't find this too surprising, given that his call to Christ and mission included these promises from the Lord: "I will show him how much he must suffer for my name" (Acts 9:16). Shortly after Paul's conversion, Jews in Damascus attempted to kill him. He fled the city secretly at night (Acts 9:23–25). After Paul rejoined the apostles in Jerusalem (who were initially afraid of him), Greek-speaking Jews attempted to kill him, which prompted Paul to leave for his hometown of Tarsus (Acts 9:28–30).

Sent off by the church at Antioch (Acts 13:1–3), Paul and his team headed out for the first of three missionary journeys recorded by Luke in Acts. Arriving at Pisidian Antioch (Acts 13:13–52) where many expressed interest in their gospel message, Luke writes: "the Jewish leaders incited the God-fearing women of high standing and the leading men of the city. They stirred up persecution against Paul and Barnabas, and expelled them from their region" (Acts 13:50). Continuing to Iconium (Acts 14:1–7), they preached and encountered interested hearers, but Jews and gentiles together conspired to stone them, which forced them to move on to Lystra and Derbe (Acts 14:8–20). Again, after an initial

---

5. See further Schnabel, *Paul the Missionary*, 72.

favorable hearing in Lystra, Luke records: "some Jews came from Antioch and Iconium and won the crowd over. They stoned Paul and dragged him outside the city, thinking he was dead. But after the disciples had gathered around him, he got up and went back into the city. The next day he and Barnabas left for Derbe" (Acts 14:19–20).

Paul encountered even more hardship during his second missionary journey. In Philippi (Acts 16:16–40), Paul and Silas prayed for a slave girl who had worked as a fortune teller, delivering her from demonic oppression. Angry about their impending financial loss, the girls' owners had Paul and Silas brought before the Roman magistrates, where they are beaten with rods and thrown into prison. As they sang hymns in prison, an earthquake erupted, breaking open the doors. Remaining in the prison and convincing the jailer not to take his own life, Paul and Silas went to his home, where their wounds were cared for and they were shown hospitality. The jailer and his family believed the gospel.

As Paul ministers in Thessalonica (Acts 17:1–15), jealous Jews incite "bad men" to start a riot in the city. Since Paul and his companions could not be located, the mob went after Jason, the leader of a house church in the city. When the team continues to Berea, they receive a good and reasonable reception until Jews from Thessalonica arrive, "agitating the crowds and stirring them up" (Acts 17:13).

After the third missionary journey, Paul returns to Jerusalem (Acts 21:27—23:22). As he enters the temple to worship, Jews from Asia recognize him and falsely accuse him of taking Greeks into the temple. Rioting ensues. Protected from the mob by a Roman commander, Paul addresses the crowd, sharing his testimony and proclaiming Christ. This causes the crowd to want to harm him even more. Though spared from being flogged by the Roman commander because Paul was a Roman citizen, Paul appears before the Sanhedrin, who plot to kill him.

In the final chapters of Acts (Acts 24–25), Paul stands before the Roman Governor Felix in Caesarea, where he ends up spending two years in prison. He later goes before Governors Festus and Agrippa before appealing to Caesar and being transferred to Rome. Luke closes his narrative with Paul under house arrest in Rome (Acts 28:17–31).

Affirming Luke's narrative of his mission through suffering, Paul spoke of sharing "abundantly in the sufferings of Christ" (2 Cor 1:5), filling up in his flesh "what is still lacking in regard to Christ's afflictions" (Col 1:24), and bearing on his body "the marks of Jesus" (Gal 6:17). He added that Christ's power was "made perfect in weakness" (2 Cor 12:9) and that "for Christ's sake, I delight in weaknesses, in insults, in hardships, in persecutions, in difficulties. For when I am weak, then I am strong" (2 Cor 12:10). In a concrete summary of his hardships in mission that parallels Luke's account in Acts, Paul continues:

> I have worked much harder, been in prison more frequently, been flogged more severely, and been exposed to death again and again. Five times I received from the Jews the forty lashes minus one. Three times I was beaten with rods, once I was pelted with stones, three times I was shipwrecked, I spent a night and a day in the open sea, I have been constantly on the move. I have been in danger from rivers, in danger from bandits, in danger from my fellow Jews, in danger from Gentiles; in danger in the city, in danger in the country, in danger at sea; and in danger from false believers. I have labored and toiled and have often gone without sleep; I have known hunger and thirst and have often gone without food; I have been cold and naked. (2 Cor 11:23–27)

According to church tradition, after another stint in prison, Paul was beheaded in Rome in AD 68, bringing to a close a remarkable journey of itinerant preaching, church planting, and suffering for the gospel.

Christian Martyrdom

Suffering in Hebrews, Peter, Revelation

Beyond Acts, other New Testament authors affirmed that the first-century church continued to suffer. The author of Hebrews describes hardship on a number of levels:

> Remember those earlier days after you had received the light, when you endured in a great conflict full of suffering. Sometimes you were publicly exposed to insult and persecution; at other times you stood side by side with those who were so treated. You suffered along with those in prison and joyfully accepted the confiscation of your property, because you knew that you yourselves had better and lasting possessions. (Heb 10:32–34)[6]

Peter addresses scattered believers in "Pontus, Galatia, Cappadocia, Asia and Bithynia" facing grief "in all kinds of trials" (1 Pet 1:1; 5:6). Schnabel asserts that their hardship came primarily in the form of slander and verbal abuse.[7]

Finally, in Revelation, a work written during the reign of the persecuting Emperor Domitian (rex, 81–96), John emphasizes the battle between Christ and the evil one, and that the church was God's suffering agent in mission (Rev 2:1—3:22; 12:5; 19:15). In Smyrna, some believers had been denounced by the Jews—an action that could lead to imprisonment or death (Rev 2:9–10). In Pergamon, a believer named Antipas was put to death for his faith (Rev 2:13). Finally, John's heavenly vision in the opening of the seals included discovering "those who had been slain because of the word of God and the testimony they had maintained" (Rev 6:9).[8]

Based on this short summary of the suffering first-century church, there are only a few Roman provinces where persecution

---

6. See further Schnabel, "The Persecution of Christians in the First Century," 536–37.

7. See further Schnabel, "The Persecution of Christians in the First Century," 544.

8. See further Flemming, *Contextualization in the New Testament*, 281–82; also Schnabel, "The Persecution of Christians in the First Century," 544–45.

did *not* occur—Cyprus, Cilicia (Paul's home province), Pamphylia, and possibly Spain and Egypt. Those who persecuted early Christians included Jewish leaders and mobs, Roman officials, and also prominent men and women in various cities. Their means of oppressing the church included verbal abuse, inciting hostility, arrests, beatings, stoning, imprisonment, expulsions, and executions.[9] For the New Testament church, suffering, persecution, and even martyrdom were normal parts of their experience following Christ.

The Suffering Church in the Roman Empire

The Romans accused the church of impiety and disrespect towards Roman pagan belief and practice. In failing to honor the many deities of the Roman pantheon, which often included the emperor, Christians were accused of atheism—worshipping a god that they could not see. The Romans believed that this lack of devotion would anger the gods, who would then remove their protection from Rome. Tertullian of Carthage (ca. 160–ca. 220) reacted strongly to these claims:

> They think the Christians the cause of every public disaster, of every affliction with which the people are visited. If the Tiber rises as high as the city walls, if the Nile does not send its waters up over the fields, if the heavens give no rain, if there is an earthquake, if there is famine or pestilence, straightway the cry is, "Away with the Christians to the lion!"[10]

Though sarcastic, Tertullian's remarks capture the motivations of pagan mobs and some emperors, in whose mind's religion was tied to the empire's economic, political, and military health. In the mindset of many Romans, being Roman meant honoring the gods

---

9. See further Schnabel, "The Persecution of Christians in the First Century," 546–47.

10. Tertullian, *Apology* 40 (*ANF* 3.48).

of the Roman pantheon. Not doing this was considered dangerous impiety.

Building on this religious motivation, the Roman government condemned Christianity in a legal sense as an unlawful sect. Legislation was carried out in an uneven manner. As we will show, at times local governors ruled against Christians to calm angry mobs. At other times, some Roman emperors issued decrees that were intended to be carried out throughout whole empire. Roman officials reacted to the church's exclusive faith-claims about Christ and the rejection of the Roman pantheon's plurality of gods. In addition to charges of atheism, the Roman authorities charged the Christians with cannibalism and sexual immorality because of pagan misunderstandings about the Eucharist and agape feasts. Finally, Christians were deemed unlawful because they were simply members of a new religion. Though the Jews were not always appreciated, they never received this illegal status thanks to their antiquity.

The early church endured sporadic periods of discrimination and suffering from its beginnings until the early fourth century.[11] Beginning around 64, the Emperor Nero (rex, 54–68) persecuted Christians in Rome. Domitian (rex, 81–96) did the same toward the end of the first century. This pattern of discrimination, which at times included violence, continued until just before Constantine (rex, 312–37) came to power in the early fourth century.

Most anti-Christian actions were carried out on a local level. In many cases, angry pagan mobs, frustrated at the perceived impiety that divided families and threatened society, initiated proceedings against Christians before local governors. Because most Roman governors oversaw vast territories, they often made hasty judgments, largely in the interest of maintaining order. This scenario explains the famous trials of Polycarp in Smyrna (Asia) in 156 and the martyrs of Lyons in 177. It also provides a context for understanding the Bithynian (Asia Minor) governor Pliny's (rex,

---

11. See further Wilken, *First Thousand Years*, 65–71; Moss, *Ancient Christian Martyrdom*, 12; Kalantzis, *Caesar and the Lamb*, 11, 25, 149; Frend, *Martyrdom and Persecution*, 238–42, 285–323, 351–92.

111–13) appeal in 112 to the Emperor Trajan (rex, 98–117) for advice in dealing with accused Christians. He asked: Should people be treated differently according to age? Does recanting constitute a pardon? Is merely professing to be a Christian a crime? Trajan responded:

> You have adopted the proper course . . . in your examination of the cases of those who were accused to you as Christians, for indeed nothing can be laid down as a general ruling involving something like a set form of procedure. They are not to be sought out; but if they are accused and convicted, they must be punished.[12]

If Christians were not to be pursued, how could they be convicted and punished? Trajan's crafty and ambiguous response, which became the official imperial policy for a century and a half, contributed to further mob-instigated discrimination and violence.

Though anti-Christian actions occurred largely on a local level, some Roman emperors took measures against the church from the highest level. In 202, Septimius Severus (rex, 193–211), the first Roman emperor from Africa, enacted a law forbidding conversion to Judaism and Christianity. Later, in 249, Decius (rex, 249–51) launched an empire-wide campaign to revive traditional Roman religion. Part of his strategy included rooting out anti-Roman, atheistic sects such as the Christians. In 249, the government issued an initial decree, ordering all church leaders to offer sacrifices to the Roman deities and to lead their congregations to do the same. The following year, administrators were dispatched to every Roman province to enforce an order for a universal sacrifice to the Roman gods. Many Christians obeyed the order and received a certificate for their sacrifices. Some managed to secure a certificate by bribing the officials, while others, including some church leaders, refused altogether and paid with their lives. The Decian persecution ended in 251 when the emperor was killed in battle.

---

12. Trajan, *Letter* 10.97 (Stevenson, *A New Eusebius*, 16).

Beginning in 257, Valerian (rex, 253-60) initiated a similar campaign. The government initially demanded a sacrifice from all Roman citizens and targeted church leaders. Christian worship assemblies and funerals were also banned. Unhappy with the response, the emperor ordered the execution of resistant clergy and laymen, confiscated church members' property, and purged the Roman Senate of all Christians. In 260, Valerian was killed in battle against the Persians; and the following year, his son and successor, Gallienus (rex, 260-68), issued an edict of toleration, beginning forty years of peace for Christians in the empire.

Also motivated to revive Roman paganism, the Emperor Diocletian (rex, 284-305) launched what has been called the Great Persecution in 303. In the first of four edicts, the government ordered churches closed, banned worship services, seized Scriptures, and targeted influential Christians in society. In the second edict, clergy were forced to sacrifice or face imprisonment; while in the third, they were threatened with torture and execution. In a final act, all citizens in the empire were commanded to sacrifice or face death. Ironically, in this last stage, some members of Diocletian's own family and his counselors—professing Christians—were arrested and executed. Following Diocletian's abdication in 305, Galerius (rex, 305-11) continued suppressing Christians in the eastern part of the empire until 311. Constantius (rex, 293-306), the western emperor and Constantine's father, chose not to enforce the suppressing edicts in his domain. On his deathbed in 311, Galerius overturned the edicts. When Constantine came to power in 312, he continued Galerius' policy and gave peace to the church in the empire.

Christian persecution occurred in a sporadic, uneven manner around the Roman Empire, and oppression largely took place at the local levels of society. Many believers in the Roman Empire in the first four centuries would have considered suffering and persecution as a normal part of their Christian faith.

Monks: The New Martyrs

During the fourth century, an intriguing new Christian movement known as monasticism developed.[13] Following Christ's model, after their baptisms, monks followed the Lord into the wilderness. Their ascetic vocation remained anchored at the foot of the cross.[14] While monastic practices may be traced to Jesus, Paul, and other first-century Christians,[15] monks also emerged in the fourth century as a response to the church's increasingly favored status in the Roman Empire. Roger Goehring argues that martyrdom had been the "ultimate expression of Christian commitment" in the Roman context in the first three centuries; however, following the rise of Constantine and the peace and favor given to the church, "the monk replaced the martyr as a Christian hero" and "they became the earthly embodiment of the heavenly communion of saints."[16] Because of their ascetic commitment and deliberate identification with Christ's sufferings and death, in a spiritual sense, monks became the new "martyrs."

Renouncing the world, these men and women embraced voluntary poverty and celibacy. Their daily lives largely revolved around the three major disciplines of prayer, reading and studying Scripture, and manual labor. Monks prayed individually, in groups, during liturgical assemblies, and as they went about their work. Prayer was facilitated not only through the discipline of fasting but also through work, which helped the monk focus while praying. They read Scripture and sang psalms individually, in groups, and during worship gatherings. Finally, monks worked not just to stay focused in prayer but also to sustain themselves and their

---

13. The term monk comes from two words—*monos* ("alone") and *monachos* ("solitary one")—while monasticism comes from *monasterion*, the monk's individual cell or the monastery where a group of monks lived together. See further Goehring, "Monasticism," 769; Harmless, *Desert Christians*, 459, 493; and Dunn, *Emergence of Monasticism*, 1.

14. See further Gesko, "Early Monasticism and the Search for Friendship with God."

15. See further, Peters, *The Monkhood of All Believers*, 1–20.

16. Goehring, "Monasticism," 769.

community. Over time, various monastic rules were developed to give guidance for daily ascetic living.

Though monasticism was based on these common values, the movement was also diverse. On one end of the spectrum, anchoritic monasticism emphasized the "extreme solitary life."[17] Spiritual growth and victory over the flesh happened best through withdrawal into isolation. On the other end of the spectrum, in coenobitic or communal monasticism "monks lived together in a community under a common monastic rule."[18] Though withdrawing from the world, this group believed that community with other monks was necessary for spiritual growth. Over time, the coenobitic approach became the dominant form of Christian monasticism. Finally, a group called semi-hermitic monks combined elements of both anchoritic and coenobitic monasticism.

Several figures stand out in the development of monasticism and are worthy of mention. Antony (ca. 251–ca. 356) became a prominent symbol of anchoritic monasticism because of the publication of Athanasius' *Life of Antony*. Antony was drawn to an ascetic lifestyle when he heard Jesus' words: "If you want to be perfect, go, sell your possessions and give to the poor, and you will have treasure in heaven. Then come, follow me" (Matt 19:21). Taking the text literally, he sold his possessions and gave what he had to the poor, while also providing for his sister's material needs. Initially, he moved to the edge of his village before relocating across the Nile to a more remote area to avoid human contact. Ironically, his withdrawal seemed to invite more and more pilgrims and visitors, which forced him farther into the wilderness near the Red Sea. After twenty years living in isolation, he became the spiritual father of a loosely-related group of anchorites.[19]

Of all the people who could be credited with the development of communal monasticism none deserves more credit than Pachomius (292–348). After his discharge from the Roman army,

17. Goehring, "Monasticism," 770.

18. Goehring, "Monasticism," 770.

19. See further Goehring, "Monasticism," 771; and Dunn, *Emergence of Monasticism*, 2, 8–12.

he returned home to Upper Egypt, where he was converted and began living in an ascetic manner. He formed a community of monks at Tabenessi. This later expanded into other settlements down the Nile River in Upper Egypt, which grew to include as many as three thousand monks. Pachomius organized monastic settlements into what he called the *koinonia* ("fellowship"). Each settlement contained as many as forty houses and had leaders for individual houses and the overall settlement. Pachomius' organizational structure, probably inherited from his training in the Roman military, facilitated both leadership development, and growth of the overall *koinonia*. He also drafted the first known monastic rule. This manual expressed the values of the *koinonia* and served as a guide for how those in the community would carry out their daily lives.[20]

Influenced toward ascetic living by his own family, Basil of Caesarea (329–79) served in Asia Minor. A coenobitic monk and ordained bishop, Basil articulated a monastic rule in his *Longer Rules* and *Shorter Rules*. He considered community a necessary means for spiritual growth. Basil's monastic theology was probably best summarized by Christ's teaching, "Love your neighbor as yourself" (Matt 22:39). He critiqued monks who were so focused on the contemplative aspects of the ascetic life that they ignored opportunities to minister others.[21]

John Cassian (360–435) served as a broker between eastern and western Christianity. As such, he influenced western monasticism with Egyptian values. Born in Scythia Minor (modern Bulgaria and Romania), Cassian lived among the Egyptian monks and recorded their dialogues in his work *Conferences*, which presented an anchoritic monastic vision. He also authored *Institutes* that outlined the coenobitic approach. Cassian was probably influenced by Basil and Pachomius' thoughts on communal monasticism through reading their rules and other writings. He spent the latter

---

20. See further Smither, *Augustine as Mentor*; Dunn, *Emergence of Monasticism*, 25–27; and Harmless, *Desert Christians*, 115.

21. See further Harmless, "Monasticism," 496, 505; and Dunn, *Emergence of Monasticism*, 38–39, 70.

part of his life in Gaul (France), establishing monasteries in Marseille.²² Cassian likened monastic obedience—to one's superior and brothers—to martyrdom.²³

Often remembered for his work as a theologian, Augustine of Hippo (354–430) served as a monk-bishop in North Africa. A contemporary of Cassian, he developed the first monastic rule in the western church and trained clergy for ministry in the African church from his clergy monastery in Hippo. Augustine's monastic labor included preaching, teaching, and writing theology for the church.²⁴

Finally, the most famous monastic innovator in the western tradition was Benedict of Nursia (ca. 480–547). Originally a cave-dwelling hermit, Benedict embraced the communal approach and founded a monastery at Monte Cassino near Rome in 529. Influenced by Antony, Pachomius, Basil, Augustine, and Cassian, Benedict developed his own rule that focused on prayer and liturgy. Specifically, Benedict set a daily schedule for prayer and singing psalms, reading Scripture, and work. More than any other monastic leader before him, Benedict brought balance and moderation to monastic living.²⁵ As part of his teaching on humility, Benedict called his monks to "quietly embrace suffering." Citing a litany of Scripture from the Psalms, the Gospels, and Paul, Benedict argued that monks truly obey the Lord when they prove "patient amid hardships and unjust treatment."²⁶

Through their commitment to spiritual disciplines such as prayer, fasting, work, celibacy, and living in community with others, monks embraced suffering and became a new type of "martyr." As their spiritual fortitude developed, monks also served as

---

22. See further Goehring, "Monasticism," 774; also Dunn, *Emergence of Monasticism*, 74–81, 88–89; and Harmless, "Monasticism," 495.

23. See further Holzherr, *Rule of Benedict*, 159.

24. See further Smither, *Augustine as Mentor*, 134–57; Dunn, *Emergence of Monasticism*, 64, 85–88; and Harmless, "Monasticism," 496.

25. See further Goehring, "Monasticism," 774; Dunn, *Emergence of Monasticism*, 114, 128, 173, 192; and Harmless, *Desert Christians*, 373.

26. *Rule of Benedict* 7.35, 42 (pp. 140–41).

the primary agents of cross-cultural global mission between the fourth and sixteenth centuries.[27]

Medieval and Modern Voices

Franciscans

One medieval monastic order, the Franciscans or Friars Minor ("little brothers"), was founded as a direct result of the conversion, vision, and ministry of Francis of Assisi (1182–1226). The son of a wealthy Italian textile merchant, Francis was embroiled in Italy's civil war as a young man. Enduring capture and imprisonment, Francis rethought his life, converted, and eventually became a monk. Striving to imitate Christ through voluntary poverty, preaching, and caring for the poor, Francis quickly attracted a community of brothers. In 1216, the pope officially recognized the Franciscan order.[28]

From an early point in their history, the Franciscans engaged in cross-cultural mission work. Particularly burdened to "preach the Christian faith and penance to the Saracens [Muslims]," Francis set sail for the Holy Land in 1212 but never made it because of a shipwreck.[29] Later, he attempted to go to Spain and meet with the Muslim leader of Morocco but was prevented by illness. Francis finally realized his dream of preaching the gospel to Muslims in 1219 when he accompanied the Christian armies to Egypt as a chaplain. There, he crossed enemy lines to meet with the Egyptian Sultan Malik al-Kamil (ca. 1177–1238), proclaiming the Christian message to him.[30]

---

27. See further, Smither, *Missionary Monks*.

28. See Francis, *The Rule* 6.4; also Lawrence, *The Friars*, 34.

29. Thomas of Celano, *Life of Francis* 20.55 in Cusato, "Francis and the Franciscan Movement," 24.

30. See Daniel, "Franciscan Missions," 241–42; Lawrence, *The Friars*, 37–38, 43–46; Moorman, *History of the Franciscan Order*, 24–25, 30–31, 62–74, 166–69, 227–29; Cusato, "Francis and the Franciscan Movement," 25–27; and McMichael, "Francis and the Encounter with the Sultan," 128.

Christian Martyrdom

Francis's mission to Muslims demonstrated two significant values. First, his initiative toward Muslims fulfilled a longing that he had for martyrdom. This was his motivation in the initial attempt to sail to the Holy Land in 1212 and also to the Egyptian sultan in 1219. When he learned of the deaths of five Friars Minor, who had been sent to Morocco to preach to Muslims, Francis praised their memories and declared that he *truly* had five brothers.[31]

Second, though Francis longed for martyrdom, his posture toward Muslims and non-believers in general was one of peace. In a section of his *Earlier Rule,* arguably written after Francis' visit to the sultan, he wrote:

> All my brothers: Let us pay attention to what the Lord says: Love your enemies and do good to those who hate you, for our Lord Jesus Christ, whose footprints we must follow, called his betrayer a friend and willingly offered himself to his executioners. Our friends, therefore, are all those who unjustly inflict upon us distress and anguish, shame and injury, sorrow and punishment, martyrdom and death. We must love them greatly, for we shall possess eternal life because of what they bring us.[32]

Francis instructed the brothers to serve among Muslims with peace and humility and to avoid arguments and disputes while preaching the gospel. Clearly, Francis illustrated these values during his encounter with the sultan: he refrained from attacking Islam or the prophet Muhammad and focused on proclaiming the gospel and praying for the sultan. Interestingly, Francis received safe passage to the sultan's camp and was returned safely at the conclusion of their discussions.[33]

While embracing voluntary poverty and hardship as monks, Francis and the brothers faced the possibility of martyrdom in

---

31. See Robson, "Writings of St. Francis," 46–47; also Daniel, "Franciscan Missions," 244; and Lawrence, *The Friars,* 204.

32. Francis, *Earlier Rule* 22 in McMichael "Francis and the Encounter with the Sultan," 134.

33. See Francis, *Rule* 3, 11–12; Francis, *Admonitions* 1, 15; also Daniel, "Franciscan Missions," 242–43; McMichael, "Francis and the Encounter with the Sultan," 128–35; and Short, "The *Rule* and the Life," 55, 61.

their mission work among Muslims. In Francis' case, the peaceful posture he demonstrated before the sultan probably saved his life.

Moravians

In the early eighteenth century, the German nobleman Nicolaus Ludwig von Zinzendorf (1700–1760) abandoned his career in public service to become a Christian minister. He had been influenced by a German movement known as the Pietists—a group committed to experiencing Christian life and teaching on a heart level. Zinzendorf and his wife adopted an ascetic lifestyle built around prayer and studying the Scriptures. Though they were wealthy, they chose to live very simply.[34]

In 1722, Zinzendorf opened his estate at Berthelsdorf in Saxony, later renamed *Hernhutt* ("the Lord's watch"), to Protestant refugees fleeing religious oppression in neighboring Moravia. The diverse community of carpenters, craftsmen, and shoemakers constructed dwellings and shops while striving to live in Christian community. Five years into the experiment, the Moravians experienced an apparent spiritual revival, which prompted them to begin an around-the-clock prayer meeting that lasted for one hundred years.

In this environment of renewal, the community set their sights on the spiritual needs of the world. In 1732, the Moravian Church began sending its first missionaries around the globe. Building from their Pietist roots, proclaiming a gospel of love was central to their mission focus. Also, since many Moravians already worked as carpenters and artisans, they continued to use these skills to support themselves on the field. During this period, a high percentage of Moravian believers—about one in sixty—served as cross-cultural missionaries.

In the eighteenth century, Moravian missionaries ventured to the East and West Indies, Greenland, North America, Suriname, and South Africa. A number of them ministered amid significant

---

34. See further Terry and Gallagher, *Encountering the History of Missions*, 199–203.

hardships. In order to get close to African slaves on the sugarcane plantations in St. Thomas (Virgin Islands), John Dober (1706–66) and David Nitschmann (ca. 1695–1772) sold themselves as indentured servants. Christian David (1690–1751) endured the difficult conditions of Greenland to preach the gospel to the Greenlandic Eskimo people. He also clashed with another Lutheran missionary who accused the Moravians of peaching a sentimental gospel that did not require moral change. While serving among Native Americans in the Hudson River Valley and establishing a discipleship community in Pennsylvania, David Zeisberger (1721–1808) saw many of his disciples massacred by Patriot troops during the American Revolution.[35]

Similar to the early church and medieval monastic orders, Zinzendorf and the Moravians adopted an ascetic lifestyle of self-denial coupled with a commitment to prayer, Scripture, and manual labor. Embracing hardship, they also pursued very difficult and even dangerous mission fields where they proclaimed the gospel.

Summary

From this survey of the church in the New Testament, early Roman Empire, and through monks and later voices, we see that suffering has been a central ongoing quality of the Christian experience. The New Testament and early Roman Christians expected and often embraced suffering. Monks and later groups such as the Moravians seemed to welcome suffering in their call to take the gospel to the ends of the earth.

As believers in the global church today continue to suffer from oppressive governments, family pressure, and even violence, their experience further aligns them with the suffering church from history we have briefly reviewed. Capturing this spirit, an Egyptian Coptic priest asserted: "Every Christian must have a cross—a real one and a symbolic one, and both must be present. Every Christian must live the life of Jesus anew. Christians

---

35. See further Hutton, *History of the Moravian Church*, 217–20; and Tucker, *From Jerusalem to Irian Jaya*, 100–113.

in Egypt have always understood this, and that is why Christianity is so strong in Egypt."[36] By contrast, the modern church in the West—blessed with comfort and prosperity—becomes the unrecognizable character in our sketch of church history so shaped by suffering and hardship.

Because we worship a Suffering Servant, the Christian life is about suffering. From this basis we now turn to sketch out three themes and outcomes of martyrdom: witness, raising a prophetic voice, and worship.

---

36. Mosebach, *The 21: A Journey into the Land of the Coptic Martyrs*, 130.

3

In Martyrdom We Witness

By definition, a martyr is a *witness*. The New Testament speaks about the act of witnessing *(martyreō)* and the person who witnesses *(martys)*. So it might seem strange to dedicate an entire chapter to martyrs being witnesses. However, in this chapter we emphasize the verbal witness given by those who suffered and died for the faith. To be a witness means to open our mouths at some point and proclaim the gospel—the death, burial, and resurrection of Jesus—and to invite friends and enemies to follow Jesus.

In this chapter, focusing largely on the early church period, we encounter martyrs who refused to deny their faith amid pressures, trials, and imprisonment. We meet others who clearly proclaimed their faith during these public settings, including some who communicated the gospel in an almost creedal fashion. Finally, we discuss briefly the emergence of Christian apologetics as an explanation of Christian faith in the face of misunderstandings, false accusations, and persecution.

Confessing Christ

Many early Christians in the first three centuries verbally shared their faith during their arrest and court proceedings. These testimonies have been captured in accounts such as the acts of the martyrs *(acta)* or martyrdoms *(passio)*, which were preserved and transmitted by the early church.

On one level, verbal witness included the simple confession of being a Christian. In the famous martyrdom account of Polycarp of Smyrna (d. 155), the bishop defended his refusal to make the pagan sacrifice by stating, "For eighty and six years I have been his servant, and he has done me no wrong, and how can I blaspheme my king who saved me?" The governor prosecuted him based on his testimony: "Polycarp has confessed that he is a Christian."[1]

In the mid-second century in neighboring Pergamum (Asia Minor), Carpus (d. 250) responded to the order to sacrifice by stating, "I am a Christian . . . and I venerate Christ the Son of God. . . . I will not sacrifice to such idols as these. . . . May the gods be destroyed who have not made heaven and earth." His fellow martyr Papylus added, "I have served Christ from my youth and I have never offered sacrifice to idols. I am a Christian."[2]

Second- and third-century North African martyrs responded similarly. Speratus, one of the Scillitan martyrs (d. 180), declared during his trial: "I do not recognize the empire of this world. Rather, I serve that God whom no man has seen, nor can see, with these eyes." When questioned by the authorities, each member of the group confessed, "I am a Christian," which became the concluding evidence for their condemnation.[3] When asked by the governor of Carthage if she was a Christian, Perpetua (d. 203) replied, "Yes, I am."[4] During his trial, exile, and eventual execution in Carthage, Bishop Cyprian (d. 258) testified: "I am a Christian and a bishop. I recognize no other gods but the one true God who made heaven and earth, and the sea, and that that is in them."[5]

---

1. *Martyrdom of Polycarp*, 8, 9, 12. Unless otherwise noted, all English translations of these are other acts are from Mursurillo, *Acts of the Christian Martyrs*.
2. *Acts of Carpus, Papylus, and Agathonicê*.
3. *Acts of the Scillitan Martyrs*.
4. *Passion of Perpetua and Felicitas*, 3, 5–6.
5. *Acts of Cyprian*, 1, 3.

During the Decian persecution in the mid-third century, Pionius of Smyrna (d. ca. 250) was arrested and ordered by the Roman officials to eat meat sacrificed to idols. When taken into the theatre where he would be burned alive and where his trial became much more public, Pionius repeatedly confessed: "I am a Christian . . . [I worship] the God who is almighty . . . who made the heaven and the earth and all things that are in them."[6]

Clarifying the Gospel

During their trials, a number of martyrs went beyond this simple confession of faith and sought to clarify aspects of the gospel. Responding to the Prefect Rusticus' queries about the nature of his faith, Justin Martyr (d. 165) testified:

> I have committed myself to the true doctrines of the Christians, . . . the belief that we piously hold regarding the God of the Christians, whom alone we hold to be the craftsman of the whole world from the beginning, and also regarding Jesus Christ, the child of God, who was foretold by the prophets as one who was to come down to mankind as a herald of salvation and teacher of good doctrines.[7]

In his late second-century trial, Apollonius (d. 185) declared, "Yes, I am a Christian . . . and hence I worship and fear the God who made heaven and earth, the sea and all that is in them." Just prior to his execution, he continued with a confession about the person of Christ:

> Jesus Christ, he who was our Savior . . . became man in Judea; he was righteous in all things and was filled with divine wisdom. Lovingly did he teach us who was the God of all things, and what was the purpose of virtue in a life of holiness, adapting his words to the minds of men. By his passion he destroyed the roots of sin . . . to worship the immortal God alone, to believe that the soul is

---

6. *Martyrdom of Pionius the Presbyter and his Companions*, 7–9, 15–16.
7. *Acts of Justin and Companions*, 2.

immortal, to be convinced that there will be a judgment after death, and that there will be a reward given by God after the resurrection.[8]

During the Great Persecution under the Emperor Diocletian, Julius (d. ca. 304), a Roman army veteran, refused to burn incense to the emperor, confessing, "I am a Christian." He continued by proclaiming Christ and inviting his hearers to believe: "It was he [Jesus] who died for our sins... in order to give us eternal life. This same man Christ is God and abides forever and ever. Whoever believes in him will have eternal life; and whoever denies him will have eternal punishment."[9]

Apologetics

Persecution and martyrdom allowed some Christians the opportunity to bring a defense of the faith against Jewish, heretical, and pagan thought. Justin wrote his *First Apology* in the mid-second century around the time of Polycarp's execution. Fashioning the document in the form of a Roman court appeal *(biblidion)*, he addressed it to the Emperor Antoninus Pius and his sons.[10] Justin challenged the unlawful practice of persecuting Christians without examining their behavior. He indirectly challenged the logic of the Emperor Trajan's policy of not hunting down Christians but then prosecuting them when they were brought before the authorities by the mob.[11] He asserted that Christians were truly the best citizens of the Roman Empire.

Answering charges that Christians were atheists, cannibals, and sexually immoral, Justin explained that Christians worshipped an invisible God, that the Lord's Supper was a memorial to Christ's broken body and shed blood, and that agape feasts were

---

8. *Martyrdom of the Saintly and Blessed Apostle Apollonius, also called Sakeas.*

9. *Martyrdom of Julius the Veteran*, 1–3.

10. Justin, *First Apology*, 2.

11. Justin, *First Apology*, 3, 5.

an occasion for Christian fellowship. Justin added that Christianity was a rational faith and that Roman paganism was actually the irrational belief system.[12]

Around 177, Justin's disciple Athenagoras addressed his *Plea for the Christians* to the Emperor Marcus Aurelius and his son Commodus. He opens with the complaint: "Although we do no wrong . . . you allow us to be harassed, plundered, and persecuted, the mob making war on us only because of our name."[13] Appealing to Marcus' interest in philosophy, Athenagoras asserted that the God of the Scriptures was the true God intricately related to the universe. He added that the best Hellenistic philosophers were also monotheists.

Like Justin, Athenagoras answered the pagan charges of atheism:

> We are not atheists since we acknowledge one God, who is uncreated, eternal, invisible, impassible, incomprehensible, illimitable. He is grasped only by mind and intelligence, and surrounded by light, beauty, spirit, and indescribable power. By him the universe was created through his Word, was set in order and is held together.[14]

He responded to the charge that Christians were immoral by citing Jesus' teachings from the Sermon on the Mount, especially about refraining from looking at women lustfully. Finally, he explained the mystery of Christ's incarnation, adding some early Christian reflection on the doctrine of the Trinity: "We acknowledge a God, and a Son, His Logos, and a Holy Spirit, united in essence—the Father, Son, the Spirit, because the Son is the Intelligence, Reason, Wisdom of the Father, and the Spirit and effluence, as light from fire."[15]

Tertullian defended the Latin-speaking African church against similar pagan claims. In his *Apology*, he defended

12. Justin, *First Apology*, 9.

13. Athenagoras, *Plea for the Christians*, 1. All quotations are from Ehrman, *After the New Testament*, 65–71.

14. Athenagoras, *Plea for the Christians*, 10.

15. Athenagoras, *A Plea for the Christians*, 24.

Christianity against the charges of incest and cannibalism, explaining how Christians conducted themselves during worship gatherings. He also ridiculed the way Christians were judged in court and were tried for simply having the name Christian. Though warning the Roman official Scapula about persecuting Christians, Tertullian emphasized the love that Christians have for their enemies:

> We have sent, therefore, this tract to you in no alarm about ourselves, but in much concern for you and for all our enemies, to say nothing of our friends. For our religion commands us to love even our enemies, and to pray for those who persecute us, aiming at a perfection all its own, and seeking in its disciples something of a higher type than the commonplace goodness of the world. For all love those who love them; it is peculiar to Christians alone to love those that hate them.[16]

Conversions and Spiritual Influence

Martyr-Inspired Conversions

In his *Second Apology,* Justin stated that he was drawn to the gospel in part because of the testimony of suffering Christians. He writes: "For I myself, too, when I was delighting in the doctrines of Plato, and heard the Christians slandered, and saw them fearless of death, and of all other-things which are counted fearful, perceived that it was impossible that they could be living in wickedness and pleasure."[17]

Tertullian was convinced that suffering and martyrdom directly resulted in conversions and church growth. In his *Apology,* he taunted the Roman authorities: "But go zealously on . . . kill us, torture us, condemn us, grind us to dust; your injustice is the proof that we are innocent, . . . the [more] often we are mown down by you, the more in number we grow; the blood of Christians is

---

16. Tertullian, *To Scapula,* 1 (*ANF* 3).
17. Justin, *Second Apology,* 12 (*ANF* 1).

seed."[18] Elsewhere he adds: "For all who witness the noble patience of its martyrs, as struck with misgivings, are inflamed with desire to examine into the matter in question; and as soon as they come to know the truth, they straightway enroll themselves its disciples."[19] Though Tertullian was given to exaggeration, we can point to instances of suffering that influenced conversions to Christ in third-century North Africa. Throughout the account of Perpetua and Felicitas and companions, the group had regular contact with people in the prison, court, and amphitheater where a Christian testimony could be given. One character of interest is the chief prison officer Pudens, who is mentioned multiple times in the *Passion of Perpetua and Felicitas*. Early in the narrative, we learn that he is impressed by the testimony of the Christians and shows them favor by allowing them more visitors.[20] Later, the narrator reports that Pudens had believed: "the head of the prison was himself a Christian."[21] The group of believers also seemed to influence the curious crowds that came to see them in the prison. The narrator records that "they spoke to the mob with the same steadfastness, warned them of God's judgment, stressing the joy they would have in their suffering, and ridiculing the curiosity of those that came to see them." The narrator concludes: "Thus everyone would depart from the prison in amazement, and many of them began to believe."[22]

Virtuous Appeal of Suffering

While some believed the gospel because of the testimony of martyrs, other pagans and non-Christians seemed more open to the Christian faith because of the virtuous appeal of Christian martyrs who suffered.

18. Tertullian, *Apology*, 50.12–14 (*ANF* 3).
19. Tertullian, *To Scapula*, 5 (*ANF* 3).
20. *Passion of Perpetua and Felicitas* 9.
21. *Passion of Perpetua and Felicitas* 16.
22. *Passion of Perpetua and Felicitas*, 17.

In the martyrdom narrative of the Spanish church leader Fructuosus (d. 259), we read: "As Bishop Fructuosus was being taken to the amphitheater with his deacons, the people began to sympathize with him, for he was much beloved of pagans and Christians alike."[23] After authorities burned Papylus and Carpus alive in Pergamum, the pagan crowd protested their treatment by exclaiming, "This is a harsh judgment and an unjust sentence."[24] Observing the torture experienced by Pionius and his companions, some onlookers sympathized, "what a terrible chastisement." Once returned to the prison, the group apparently found favor with the prison guards and were moved out of the worst section of the jail to the best part.[25]

Eusebius' (263–339) history of the martyrs of Palestine during the Diocletian persecution offers further support. Remembering the impact of a believer named Peter on the Roman officials, Eusebius writes: "Peter . . . appeared, a famous confessor of the kingdom of God; and so manfully did he behave in his struggle for the worship of God, and so victorious was he in the conflict of his martyrdom, that he even excited admiration in the judge himself."[26] Athanasius (ca. 296–373) also affirmed that suffering Palestinian Christians invited the sympathies of the pagan observers.[27]

Pagan audiences seemed especially moved by the suffering of women, who were often subjected to significant cruelty and torture.[28] In a horrific account from Palestine, Eusebius describes an unnamed virgin from the town of Baishan:

> [She] had been brought by force from Baishan, and suffered insults and cruel tortures from the judge before she was condemned. This same blessed woman he stripped

---

23. *Martyrdom of Bishop Fructuosus and his Deacons, Augurius and Eulogius*, 3.

24. Cited in Frend, *Martyrdom and Persecution*, 201.

25. *Martyrdom of Pionius the Presbyter and his Companions*, 10–11.

26. Eusebius, *History of the Martyrs in Palestine*, 38.

27. Frend, *Martyrdom and Persecution*, 380.

28. See further *Martyrdom of Potamiaena and Basilides*; *Martyrdom of Saints Agape, Irene, and Chinoe at Saloniki*; *Martyrdom of Crispina*, 3.

> naked . . . in order that he might indulge his lustful eyes in looking at the rest of her limbs; and he carried her about through the whole city, being tortured with straps; and afterwards took her before the tribunal of the governor, where with great boldness of speech she made the confession of her faith—that she was a Christian; and there also displayed her courage and patience under every kind of torture; and was afterwards delivered over by the governor to be burnt with fire. Moreover, the same judge became day by day more ferocious . . . and of this same maiden of whom it has been just spoken, and of those who on the same day were consummated by confession, orders were issued that their bodies should be devoured by animals, and be carefully guarded night and day till they should be consumed by birds.[29]

Eusebius added that because of the atrocities experienced by this woman and others that a "great sorrow and grief came even upon those who were aliens from us in the faith, because of these things which their own eyes beheld."[30]

Similarly, Felicitas and Perpetua's martyrdom in Carthage is only magnified because they were young women. Perpetua came from an affluent and well-known family in Carthage and had given birth to a child just prior to her arrest. Felicitas was her servant and managed to give birth to a child in prison. According to the *Passion*, an assistant to the prison guard was particularly moved by Felicitas' circumstances as a new mother facing execution.[31] Perhaps the cruelty of the whole story is best captured when the women were taken into the Carthage amphitheater:

> So they were stripped naked, placed in nets and thus brought out into the arena. Even the crowd was horrified when they saw that one was a delicate young girl and the other was a woman fresh from childbirth with the milk

---

29. Eusebius, *History of the Martyrs in Palestine*, 35.
30. Eusebius, *History of the Martyrs in Palestine*, 35
31. *Passion of Perpetua and Felicitas*, 15.

still dripping from her breasts. And so they were brought back again and dressed in unbelted tunics.[32]

Ironically, the crowd demonstrated a level of sympathy for the women; however, they were not moved enough to demand an end the whole unjust affair.

A woman named Blandina figured prominently among the martyrs of Lyons (177). After being tossed in prison and surviving an initial torture session in the amphitheater, Blandina was once again thrown to the beasts where she was beaten to death. W. H. C. Frend comments, "Those who watched her first tortures in the amphitheater are reported to have said 'that never among them had a woman suffered so much for so long.'"[33] Adding support to the claim that suffering could lead to spiritual openness, Frend continues: "Sometimes such thoughts proved to be the first stirrings towards acceptance of the Christian faith."[34]

The suffering of elderly Christians also seems to have impacted non-Christian observers.[35] The narrator of the *Martyrdom of Polycarp* makes a strong case for the virtuous appeal of this elderly bishop. Apparently, the police were moved by the eighty-six-year-old bishop's composure at the time of his arrest. His offer of hospitality and request for some time to pray surely strengthened his rapport with them. Finally, during his trial, the governor also seems impressed with the graceful manner in which Polycarp conducted himself in suffering.[36]

---

32. *Passion of Perpetua and Felicitas*, 20.
33. Frend, *Martyrdom and Persecution*, 7–9.
34. Frend, *Martyrdom and Persecution*, 9.
35. See further Eusebius' account of the aging martyrs Conon and Sylvanus of Gaza in *History of the Martyrs in Palestine*, 51.
36. *Martyrdom of Polycarp*, 7, 12.

Christian Martyrdom

Summary

Robin Lane Fox writes: "in the early church, martyrdoms were exceptionally public events."[37] At times believers were brought into the arena and put to death by wild beasts. In many other instances they were brought into court where they had public trials recorded by the Romans. During these events, they had the opportunity to declare that they were followers of Christ, to proclaim and clarify portions of the gospel, and to offer a public defense of their faith.

Though our focus in this chapter has been on martyrs from the early church who witnessed through their words in the face of trial, global Christians today have similar opportunities. While living in North Africa, I had the joy of sharing the good news with Ahmed, who began following Christ. Excited about his new faith, Ahmed began inviting his co-workers over to his apartment for coffee and to read and discuss the Bible. At Christmas, he threw a Jesus party, inviting his friends for worship, Scripture reading, and a clear explanation of the gospel. While some of his co-workers were open to the gospel, word about Ahmed's faith also reached the local police. They confiscated his Bibles and Christian books and required him to report to the police station for questioning for two weeks straight. Forced to respond repeatedly to the same set of questions, Ahmed patiently shared his faith. One evening, every officer in the station gathered around to hear his message. The chief of police took possession of Ahmed's Bible and indicated that he would need to do his own investigation on the teachings of this book. Though Ahmed was facing discrimination for his faith, he enjoyed a verbal gospel witness.

A second example of a modern witnessing church is the Coptic Church in Egypt. Tracing its origins to the first century and the ministry of the Evangelist Mark, since the seventh century, the Copts have lived as a minority faith community in a Muslim dominated society.[38] Since the late twentieth century, Coptic Christians and places of worship have come under increasing attack by

---

37. Fox, *Pagans and Christians*, 420.
38. See further Oden, *The African Memory of Mark*.

Muslim extremists. A Coptic bishop in Upper Egypt declared, "We are the Church of Martyrs. I take no special risk when I say that not a single Copt in Upper Egypt would betray the faith."[39] Within the Coptic liturgy, Egyptian Christians recite the ancient creeds such as the Nicene Creed multiple times. Following bombing attacks in recent years, Coptic believers have gathered publicly to witness verbally by reciting the Nicene Creed.[40]

On February 15, 2015, twenty Coptic Christians (plus one more from Ghana) were beheaded by members of ISIS on the beach in Sirte, Libya. The massacre was captured in a high quality five-minute short film and then posted online. The Egyptian men were from a poor village in Upper Egypt and were working in Libya to send money home to their families. At the beginning of January 2015, they were captured and tortured for forty-three days. Each day, they were ordered to say the Islamic *shahadah* ("I declare there is no other god but Allah and Muhammad is his messenger"), but they stood firm, refusing to deny their faith in Christ. Just prior to their execution, the men were heard on film softly declaring in Arabic, "*Ya Rabbi Yessua* (O Lord Jesus)."[41] In martyrdom, they witnessed.

---

39. Mosebach, *The 21: A Journey into the Land of Coptic Martyrs*, 46.

40. See further Mosebach, *The 21: A Journey into the Land of Coptic Martyrs*, 144; also Showalter, "Egypt's Copts Chant Nicene Creed After Palm Sunday Bombings," *Christian Post*. Online: https://www.christianpost.com/news/egypts-copts-chant-nicene-creed-after-palm-sunday-bombings-standing-strong-despite-massacre.html (accessed July 2, 2019).

41. See further Mosebach, *The 21: A Journey into the Land of Coptic Martyrs*.

4

In Martyrdom We Are Prophets

> King Nebuchadnezzar, we do not need to defend ourselves before you in this matter. If we are thrown into the blazing furnace, the God we serve is able to deliver us from it, and he will deliver us from Your Majesty's hand. But even if he does not, we want you to know, Your Majesty, that we will not serve your gods or worship the image of gold you have set up. (Dan 3:16–18)

With these bold words, Shadrach, Meshach, and Abednego—dispersed Jewish believers living in Babylon—refused the king's decree to bow down to a golden image. Communicating confidence in their God while also preparing to lose their lives, they spoke defiantly and righteously to power. They demonstrated raising a prophetic voice.

In the Old Testament, prophets were set apart to speak God's truth to Israel and to the nations. They confronted evil and injustice in society and also warned of God's judgment, especially if there was no repentance. In the Gospels, Jesus likewise came announcing the kingdom of God. This announcement of good news and salvation often included a message denouncing unrighteousness and injustice. Throughout the history of Christianity, many Christians, as they faced discrimination, persecution, and even martyrdom also raised a prophetic voice. In this chapter, we cover a wider angle of church history and meet those who became prophets amid suffering and martyrdom.

Prophets in the Early Church

Justin Martyr leveraged Greek philosophy and the Roman appeals system to construct a reasonable defense of the Christian faith. However, he also concludes his *First Apology* with a warning of God's judgment, especially against political leaders who unjustly persecute the church:

> If these things seem to you to be reasonable and true, honor them; but if they seem nonsensical despise them as nonsense, and do not decree death against those who have done no wrong, as you would against enemies. For we forewarn you, that you shall not escape the coming judgment of God, if you continue in your injustice and we ourselves will invite you to do that which is pleasing to God.[1]

The aged Polycarp surrendered peacefully to the authorities and even offered them hospitality while he took some time to pray. However, when he was threatened with being burned alive, he responded strongly to his captors: "The fire you threaten me with burns merely for a time and is soon extinguished. It is clear you are ignorant of the fire of everlasting punishment and of the judgment that is to come."[2]

Before being whipped and having pikes driven through his ankles, Conon (d. 250), an elderly believer in Pamphylia, declared to the authorities: "How could you thus blaspheme against the God of all things when your breath is in his hands? . . . Do you think you can terrify me by threatening me with mere words and thus suppose you can change my mind? . . . Beware lest the Judge

---

1. Justin, *First Apology*, 68 (*ANF* 1).
2. *Martyrdom of Polycarp*, 10. Unless otherwise noted, all English translations of these are other acts are from Mursurillo, *Acts of the Christian Martyrs*.

sentence you to a Hades that is unsurpassed, a fire unquenchable forever."[3]

As they were brought into the Carthage arena to face wild beasts, Revocatus, Saturninus, and Secundulus (d. 203)—companions of Perpetua and Felicitas—took a moment to warn the pagan crowd of God's impending judgment on them.[4] Tertullian, who edited the account of this group's suffering, believed that the primary role of a church leader was to be a prophet. In a letter to Scapula, the Roman-appointed governor of Carthage, Tertullian warned him that God's judgment would also fall on those who persecuted the church.[5]

Prophets in the Post-Constantine Era

Athanasius

Though Bishop Athanasius of Alexandria (ca. 296–373) did not die as a martyr, he suffered under multiple Roman emperors because of his defense of Nicene orthodoxy. At the Council of Nicaea of 325, Athanasius, then a deacon, assisted his Bishop Alexander (250–326) in the heresy trial of Arius (256–336). For nearly a decade, Arius, a presbyter in Alexandria, had been teaching that the Son of God was created by God and was therefore distinct from the Father. The gathered bishops at Nicaea articulated a creed affirming that the Son was "eternally begotten of the Father, God from God, Light from Light, true God from true God, begotten, not made, of one Being with the Father."

Following Alexander's death, Athanasius became bishop of Alexandria and served in that role of forty-five years. However, he spent about one third of his career as bishop in exile. In the first of five exiles, Athanasius was banished in 335 for refusing the Emperor Constantine's pressure to reinstate Arius to the ministry in Egypt. In 339, Athanasius fled to Rome with other Nicene-minded

---

3. *Martyrdom of Conon*, 5.
4. *Passion of Perpetua and Felicitas*, 18.
5. Tertullian, *To Scapula* 1.

bishops due to pressure from the Arian-leaning Emperor Constantius II (rex, 337–60). In 356, while Athanasius was leading worship in the St. Theonas church, a military troop sent by the emperor surrounded the church. Athanasius managed to escape and fled into the Egyptian desert, where he sought refuge among the monks. Athanasius experienced additional exiles at the hands of the pagan Emperor Julian (rex, 360–63) and the Arian-minded Emperor Valens (rex, 364–78).

Despite the strong political pressure on him, Athanasius refused to compromise on theological orthodoxy, earning him the moniker "Athanasius against the world." His courageous presence in the church at Alexandria and during periods of exile demonstrated a prophetic posture. Accustomed to suffering and leading the church from exile, when banished by Julian in 360, he wrote: "Let us retire for a brief while, my friends; 'tis but a little cloud and soon will pass."[6]

Basil of Caesarea

Like Athanasius, Basil (329–79), the monk-bishop of Caesarea, did not die a martyr. He also clashed significantly with the Roman Emperor Valens and risked exile because of theology. Basil held firm to the Nicene Creed in the face of Valens' Arian leanings. During his time as bishop, the emperor divided Cappadocia in half, limiting Basil's influence over the churches and people in the area.

Describing the hardship that fourth-century church leaders in Asia Minor faced because of Valens, Basil's friend and fellow bishop, Gregory of Nazianzus (329–90), wrote: "Exiles, banishments, confiscations, open and secret plots, . . . those who clung to the orthodox faith, as we did, were expelled from their churches."[7] If Basil had not been so popular with the people, he probably

---

6. Cited in Davis, *First Seven Ecumenical Councils*, 102.
7. Gregory of Nazianzus, *Oration* 43.30, 36 (*NPNF* 2.7).

would have been exiled as Athanasius and others had been during this period.[8]

Basil's prophetic posture comes through in his exchange with the Roman official Modestus, who threatened the bishop because of his apparent lack of respect for the Emperor Valens:

> "Fear of what?" said Basil, "How could it affect me? . . . confiscation, banishment, torture, death. Have you no other threat?" said he, "for none of these can reach me. . . . Because . . . a man who has nothing, is beyond the reach of confiscation; unless you demand my tattered rags, and the few books, which are my only possessions. Banishment is impossible for me, who am confined by no limit of place, counting my own neither the land where I now dwell, nor all of that into which I may be hurled. . . . As for tortures, what hold can they have upon one whose body has ceased to be? . . . Death is my benefactor, for it will send me the sooner to God." Amazed at this language, the prefect said, "No one has ever yet spoken thus, and with such boldness, to Modestus." "Why, perhaps," said Basil, "you have not met . . . a bishop . . . where the interests of God are at stake, we care for nothing else, and make these our sole object."[9]

Prophets in the Protestant Reformation

Leading up to and during the Protestant Reformation in Europe, a number of reformers died as martyrs. Though at times these martyrs confronted political leaders, their prophetic posture was most often directed toward the Roman Catholic church leadership.

---

8. See further Basil, *Letters* 74–76; and Gregory of Nazianzus, *Oration* 43.56.

9. Gregory of Nazianzus, *Oration* 43.48–50 (*NPNF* 2.7).

In Martyrdom We Are Prophets

Jan Huss (1372–1415)

Born into a peasant family in southern Bohemia (modern Czech Republic), Jan Huss served as rector of Prague's Bethlehem Chapel. Influenced by the English reformer John Wyclif (1330–84), Huss became convinced that Scripture was the highest authority for the church. Proud of his home culture, Huss preached from the Bethlehem pulpit in his native Czech dialect.

Paving the way for German Reformer Martin Luther (1483–1546), Huss preached against the immoral lifestyles of the popes and clergy and railed against the sale of indulgences (payment to reduce penalty for sin). In Bethlehem Chapel, he hung wall paintings depicting the simplicity and humility of Christ in contrast to the lavish living of the popes. From Scripture, he asserted that Christ was the head of the church.

Excommunicated by his archbishop, Huss was summoned to the Council of Constance of 1415, where he believed he would have the opportunity to defend his teachings. Instead, he was burned at the stake, becoming a martyr for what would become the Protestant Reformation. Facing death, Huss stated: "I appeal to Jesus Christ, the only judge who is almighty and completely just. In his hands I plead my cause, not on the basis of false witnesses and erring councils, but on truth and justice."[10] Following his death, Huss' followers formed the Unity of the Brethren movement, which eventually became the Moravian church.[11]

---

10. Cited in "John Huss, 1369–1415, Pre-Reformation Reformer." https://www.christianitytoday.com/history/people/martyrs/john-huss.html (accessed July 20, 2019).

11. See further, "Huss, John," *Oxford Dictionary of the Christian Church*. Online: www.oxford-reference.com (accessed July 21, 2019).

Christian Martyrdom

Hugh Latimer (1485–1555) and Nicholas Ridley (1500–1555)

During the Reformation in England, a movement sparked by politics as much as theology, two martyrs defied both church and political authorities.

Hugh Latimer served as the bishop of Worcester. An advocate for reading the Bible in English, Latimer preached against the Catholic doctrine of purgatory and the use of icons in worship. When ordered by his bishop to denounce Luther's teachings, he refused. He argued that faith cannot be coerced by any form of earthly power. Latimer also preached against social injustices in English society. Ultimately, he resigned his post as bishop in opposition to the Six Articles, a document pushed by King Henry VIII (rex, 1509–47) to make the English church more Roman Catholic.

Nicholas Ridley served as a chaplain under Henry before becoming the bishop of London. Rejecting the Catholic transubstantiation view of the Eucharist (that the bread and wine literally became the body and blood of Christ), Ridley became increasingly convinced of Reformation ideas. He later assisted Archbishop Thomas Cranmer (1489–1556) in the development of the *Book of Common Prayer*, the definitive expression of Anglican theology and spirituality. On trial for heresy in 1555, Ridley was pressed by scholars from Oxford Divinity School over his views of papal authority. Ridley responded that *Christ* was head of the church.

In 1553, the Catholic queen Mary Tudor (1516–58) arrested Latimer, Ridley, and Cranmer and confined them to the Tower of London. Following their heresy trial in 1555, Latimer and Ridley were burned at the stake in Oxford. Cranmer suffered the same fate the following year.[12]

---

12. See further, "Latimer, Hugh"; "Ridley, Nicholas"; "Cranmer, Thomas," *Oxford Dictionary of the Christian Church*. Online: www.oxford-reference.com (accessed July 21, 2019).

In Martyrdom We Are Prophets

Anabaptist Martyrs

On January 21, 1525 in Zurich, Conrad Grebel baptized George Blaurock by immersion. The two then began to baptize others within their circle, launching a new Protestant movement known as the Swiss Brethren. Outsiders, including Catholic, Reformed, and state leaders, called them the Anabaptists (rebaptizers). Originally disciples of Swiss Reformer Ulrich Zwingli (1484–1531), the Swiss Brethren went beyond Zwingli in two areas: they asserted that only professing believers should be baptized, and the church should be free from the entanglements of the state.

The Anabaptists quickly became an oppressed group across Europe. In 1526, the Catholic regions of Switzerland subjected them to the death penalty. By 1528, Emperor Charles V (rex, 1519–56) also imposed the death penalty on them throughout the Holy Roman Empire, a move ratified by the Diet of Speyer of 1529. To enforce these measures, an Anabaptist police force was formed and deployed across Europe. Between 1525 and 1560, around four thousand Anabaptist Christians were put to death by imperial, Catholic, and even Reformed leaders. In 1527, Zwingli had his own disciple Felix Manz drowned for being a leader of the Swiss Brethren.

In their martyrdom, the Anabaptists assumed a prophetic posture toward both political and church leaders. Sometimes called Radical Reformers—those desiring a faith rooted in the New Testament alone—the Anabaptists identified with Christ, the cross, and Christians throughout history who suffered for their faith. They believed that the true church was not a state church but a suffering church. Though most Anabaptists were pacifists when it came to fighting and war, they were revolutionary in their rhetoric. At times, they referred to imperial, Catholic, Lutheran, and Reformed leaders as the anti-Christ. Martyred Anabaptist leaders such as Balthasar Hubmaier (1480–1528) acted in a prophetic manner through their preaching and baptizing of new believers.

Though a pacifist, Hubmaier defied imperial law and the pressures of the church.[13]

Twentieth-Century Prophets

Dietrich Bonhoeffer (1906–45)

Bonhoeffer was a German Lutheran pastor who persevered in ministry under the Nazi regime of Adolf Hitler (rex, 1933–45). Believing that the church was a community filled with the real presence of Christ, he asserted that the church could not accept the status-quo values dictated by a society. He also believed that Scripture should be read to challenge our beliefs and practices—not merely to confirm them. For Bonhoeffer, the state's role was to preserve society, while the church's was to hold the state accountable to do this work in a just manner. Bonhoeffer's prophetic leanings were also shaped during his time as a student in New York City when he observed the struggles of African-American believers and learned from their theology and social justice teaching.[14]

As Hitler's power increased, many German Christians and churches accepted the führer's Aryan race (white supremacist) teachings. For Bonhoeffer, who had worshipped with African-American Christians in New York City and international believers in England and Spain, the church ceased to be the church when it embraced nationalism. He responded by helping launch the Confessing Church and affirming the Barmen Declaration, a statement crafted by Karl Barth (1886–1968) that denounced nationalism in the church.[15] Because of his prophetic stance, Bonhoeffer fully expected to suffer:

> And while I'm working with the church opposition with all my might, it's perfectly clear to me that *this* opposition

---

13. See further Butler, "'Church under the Cross': Anabaptist Theology of Martyrdom," 299–316; and Jackson and Jackson, *On Fire for Christ: Stories of Anabaptist Martyrs*.

14. See further Tietz, *Theologian of Resistance*, 10–12, 21–24, 34, 38.

15. See further Tietz, *Theologian of Resistance*, 40–49.

is only a very temporary transitional phase on the way to an opposition of a very different kind, and that very few of those involved in this preliminary skirmish are going to be there for that second struggle. I believe that all of Christendom should be praying with us for the coming of resistance "to the point of shedding blood" and for the finding of people who can suffer it through.[16]

From 1937 to 1940, Bonhoeffer defied the Nazi government by operating an underground seminary that trained pastors for Confessing churches. In 1940, the Gestapo shut it down. Bonhoeffer's actions reflected his convictions for the Christian life and discipleship, which he captured in his famous work, *Cost of Discipleship*:

> Costly grace is the hidden treasure in the field, for the sake of which people go and sell with joy everything they have. It is the costly pearl, for whose price the merchant sells all that he has. . . . It is the call of Jesus Christ which causes a disciple to leave his nets and follow him. . . . It is costly, because it calls to discipleship; it is grace, because it calls us to follow *Jesus Christ*. It is costly, because it costs people their lives; it is grace, because it thereby makes them live. . . . Above all, grace is costly, because it was costly to God, because it costs God the life of God's Son and because nothing can be cheap to us which is costly to God.[17]

Passing up an opportunity to remain in New York City and teach, Bonhoeffer returned to Germany. Though a pacifist, his theological and ethical convictions ("extraordinary necessity")[18] led him to join a conspiracy to overthrow Hitler. In 1943, he was imprisoned for his opposition to the state. The following year he was implicated in the plot to kill Hitler. Though a prison guard offered to help him escape (he refused), Bonhoeffer was hanged on April 9, 1945. In his final words before being put to death, a message to his friend Bishop George Bell of Chichester, his prophetic voice resounded:

---

16. Cited in Tietz, *Theologian of Resistance*, 53.
17. Cited in Tietz, *Theologian of Resistance*, 61.
18. Cited in Tietz, *Theologian of Resistance*, 86.

"this is for me the end, but also the beginning. . . . I believe in the principle of our universal Christian brotherhood which rises above all national hatreds and that our victory is certain."[19]

Martin Luther King, Jr. (1929–68)

The son of a Baptist minister, Martin Luther King, Jr. was ordained to the ministry at Ebenezer Baptist Church in Atlanta in 1948. His pastoral ministry took him to Montgomery, Alabama in 1954. King's career as a civil rights activist began in 1955 when he helped organize the Montgomery bus boycott, following Rosa Parks' refusal to give up her seat (in the colored section of the bus) to a white passenger. Because of this resistance, the city of Montgomery eventually integrated the public bus system.

Inspired by Christ and Mahatma Ghandi (1869–1948), King championed non-violent civil disobedience. Commenting on this approach, he wrote: "Of course, there is nothing new about this kind of civil disobedience. It was evidenced sublimely in the refusal of Shadrach, Meshach, and Abednego to obey the laws of Nebuchadnezzar, on the ground that a higher moral law was at stake." He added: "We who engage in nonviolent direction action are not the creators of tension. We merely bring to the surface the hidden tension that is already alive."[20] Because of this approach, King went to jail on numerous occasions.

At the famous march on Washington on August 28, 1962, King gave his famous "I Have a Dream" speech. Following the event, he met with President John F. Kennedy and Vice President Lyndon Johnson at the White House. Because of his work confronting racial justice, King was awarded the Nobel Peace Prize in 1964. In 1965, he organized the fifty-four-mile march from Montgomery to Selma with the aim of registering African-Americans to vote. On April 3, 1968, King visited Memphis to support striking

---

19. Cited in Tietz, *Theologian of Resistance*, 110.

20. King, *Letters from a Birmingham Jail*. Online: https://www.africa.upenn.edu/Articles_Gen/Letter_Birmingham.html (accessed July 14, 2019).

sanitation workers. The following day, April 4, he was shot to death while standing outside at the Lorraine Motel.

In addition to fighting for racial equality, the fruit of his Christian faith and pastoral ministry, King raised a prophetic voice through his preaching and public speaking. In "I Have a Dream,"[21] one of the most famous speeches in American history, he declared:

> But one hundred years later [after emancipation], the Negro still is not free. One hundred years later, the life of the Negro is still sadly crippled by the manacles of segregation and the chains of discrimination. One hundred years later, the Negro lives on a lonely island of poverty in the midst of a vast ocean of material prosperity. One hundred years later, the Negro is still languished in the corners of American society and finds himself in exile in his own land. And so we've come here today to dramatize a shameful condition.

With an urgency for justice, he continued:

> Now is the time to rise from the dark and desolate valley of segregation to the sunlit path of racial justice. Now is the time to lift our nation from the quick sands of racial injustice to the solid rock of brotherhood. Now is the time to make justice a reality for all of God's children.

He concluded the speech by casting this vision for the future:

> I have a dream that one day this nation will rise up and live out the true meaning of its creed: "We hold these truths to be self-evident, that all men are created equal." . . . And when this happens . . . we will be able to speed up that day when all of God's children, black men and white men, Jews and Gentiles, Protestants and Catholics, will be able to join hands and sing in the words of the old Negro spiritual: "Free at last! Free at last! Thank God Almighty, we are free at last!"

---

21. All excerpts from "I Have a Dream" are from: https://kinginstitute.stanford.edu/king-papers/documents/i-have-dream-address-delivered-march-washington-jobs-and-freedom (accessed July 12, 2019).

Not only did Dr. King speak prophetically to American elected officials about racial injustice and the abuses of capitalism, he criticized the white American church for its inaction. In response to a group of white ministers who urged King to wait and be patient in his activism, he drafted his famous "Letter from a Birmingham Jail." He begins with a rebuke: "Perhaps it is easy for those who have never felt the stinging darts of segregation to say, 'Wait.'" He continues: "The Negro's great stumbling block in his stride toward freedom is . . . the white moderate who is more devoted to 'order' than to justice." Lamenting the impotence of the mainstream church, he adds:

> I have looked at the South's beautiful churches with their lofty spires pointing heavenward. . . . Over and over I have found myself asking: What kind of people worship here? Who is their God? . . . If today's church does not recapture the sacrificial spirit of the early church, it will lose its authenticity, forfeit the loyalty of millions, and be dismissed as an irrelevant social club with no meaning for the twentieth century.

Martin Luther King, Jr. was martyred because of his prophetic stance against racial injustice in America. In "I've Been to the Mountaintop," King's last speech the night before he was killed, he seems to have counted the cost of his work, anticipating his untimely death at the age of thirty-nine:

> Because I've been to the mountaintop. And I don't mind. Like anybody, I would like to live a long life. Longevity has its place. But I'm not concerned about that now. I just want to do God's will. And He's allowed me to go up to the mountain. And I've looked over. And I've seen the promised land. I may not get there with you. But I want you to know tonight, that we, as a people will get to the promised land. And I'm happy tonight. I'm not worried about anything. I'm not fearing any man. Mine eyes have seen the glory of the coming of the Lord.[22]

22. All excerpts of "I've Been to the Mountaintop" are taken from: https://www.cnn.com/2018/04/04/us/martin-luther-king-jr-mountaintop-speech-trnd/index.html (accessed July 12, 2019).

In Martyrdom We Are Prophets

Oscar Romero (1917–80)

Born into a poor family in El-Salvador, Romero apprenticed as a carpenter before pursuing a call to the priesthood. While serving as archbishop of San Salvador, Romero initially resisted liberation theology and the work of priests laboring among El-Salvador's poor farming class. His perspective greatly changed when a friend and fellow priest, who was laboring for social justice, was murdered. Also, Bishop Romero became enraged at the deaths of poor children whose families did not have access to basic medical care. As a result, justice became the focal point of his ministry.

Through his weekly radio sermons, he connected with poor farmers and called for the government to stop its oppression of the Salvadoran people. During a visit to the Vatican, he shed light on his government's tyrannical ways, including torture, kidnapping, and murder. During Romero's lifetime, some seventy-five thousand Salvadorians were killed, while a million fled the country as refugees, and another million were left homeless. Because of his vocal stance against the government, he became a target for assassination. On March 24, 1980, Bishop Romero was shot and killed by agents of the Salvadoran government while leading mass.

Reminiscent of Tertullian's claim that the blood of the martyrs was seed, Romero left behind reflections on the possibility of martyrdom:

> I have frequently been threatened with death. I must say that, as a Christian, I do not believe in death but in the resurrection. If they kill me, I shall rise again in the Salvadoran people. Martyrdom is a great gift from God that I do not believe I have earned. But if God accepts the sacrifice of my life, then my blood will be like the seed of liberty, and a sign of the hope that will soon become a reality.[23]

While Romero raised a singular prophetic voice as a bishop, he also believed that the church should maintain a collective prophetic posture. He noted: "A church that doesn't provoke any crises, a

---

23. Cited in Claiborne et al., *Common Prayer*, 108–9.

gospel that doesn't unsettle, a word of God that doesn't get under anyone's skin, a word of God that doesn't touch the real sin of the society in which it is being proclaimed—what gospel is that?"[24]

Summary

Throughout Christian history, prophecy and martyrdom have walked hand in hand. From Justin and Tertullian in the early church to Bonhoeffer, Martin Luther King, Jr, and Oscar Romero in the twentieth-century church, martyrs have spoken truth to power. They have rebuked and warned non-believing political leaders. Others have confronted believing officials, too. Martyrs like Bonhoeffer called upon governments to preserve society justly. Some of these martyr-prophets also rebuked the church to return to the gospel and to pursue justice as a visible reflection of God's kingdom.

In their martyrdom, some like Dr. King called others to stand up and become prophets too. On the night before his death, he addressed ministers in the crowd at Memphis for a moment, calling them to mimic the prophets of the Old Testament: "Who is it that is supposed to articulate the longings and aspirations of the people more than the preacher? Somehow the preacher must be an Amos, and say, 'Let justice roll down like waters and righteousness like a mighty stream'" (Amos 5:24).

---

24. Cited in Claiborne et al., *Common Prayer*, 333.

5

In Martyrdom We Worship

> About midnight Paul and Silas were praying and singing hymns to God, and the other prisoners were listening to them. Suddenly there was such a violent earthquake that the foundations of the prison were shaken. At once all the prison doors flew open, and everyone's chains came loose. (Acts 16:25–26)

After being beaten and imprisoned, Paul and Silas responded with worship. As they prayed and sang hymns, God's power manifested, breaking open the prison doors and ultimately leading to the conversion of the Philippian jailer and his family.

While Paul and Silas were freed and continued to minister (until Paul was eventually martyred), many who have suffered or died as martyrs have also responded winsomely with praise and worship. In this chapter, we meet martyrs who have worshipped in their suffering or who have inspired others to worship because of their hardship.

Christian Martyrdom

Suffering, Worship, and Witness

Waodoni Mission

The mission to the Waodoni in 1955–56 became one of the most famous missionary martyr stories of the twentieth century. Five young American men (Jim Eliot, Nate Saint, Pete Fleming, Roger Youderian, and Ed McCully) and their wives sought to make peaceful contact with and evangelize a stone-aged tribe in the Ecuadorian jungle. Since their previous contact with outsiders had only been violent, the Waodoni people were also known as the Aucas ("savages").

Living among a nearby tribe and learning some of the Waodoni language, the men began to initiate friendly contract with the tribe. Thanks to Nate Saint's skills as a pilot, the men dropped off gifts to the Waodoni people. They also communicated friendly messages over a loudspeaker from above. Eventually, they scheduled a meet with the Waodoni tribesmen. After landing on a beach alongside the Curaray River in Waodoni territory on January 8, 1956, the men prayed, sang a hymn, and moved to meet the Waodoni.

Back at the mission base, a check-in radio call never came. The men had been speared to death by the people they were trying to reach with the gospel. A few days later, United States Marines found their bodies floating in the Curaray. Though the Waodoni tribesmen had initially responded peacefully to the men's overtures, they attacked them believing the men were cannibals. During the meeting, one of the men took a picture of a Waodoni woman out of his pocket attempting to build affinity. However, by pulling the woman's body out of his body he made the Waodoni believe the Americans had eaten her.

Despite the tragic murders of these young American men, Elizabeth Eliot (Jim Eliot's wife) and Rachel Saint (Nate Saint's sister) made peaceful contact with the Waodoni, accepted an invitation to live among them, and helped plant a church among the tribal people. At least one of the Waodoni men who speared the Americans on the beach believed the gospel and became a pastor in the Waodoni church and a missionary to neighboring tribes in Ecuador.[1]

Worship played a significant role in this story of missionary martyrdom. The five men worshipped and sang hymns before meeting the Waodoni. However, years after the massacre and even the establishment of the Waodoni church, it came to light that after killing the missionaries, the Waodoni tribesmen reported hearing worship—like a choir of angels—singing around them. They apparently experienced a power encounter during which they were enveloped in worship. This experience seemed instrumental in their becoming open to the missionaries' God and to believing the gospel.[2]

Mission among the Taliban

On August 3, 2001, Heather Mercer and Dayna Curry, Christian aid workers serving with the group Shelter Now, were arrested and imprisoned by the Taliban in Afghanistan. After 105 days in captivity, the women and their six co-workers were rescued by the United States military. The story of their imprisonment and rescue became front-page news in the United States.

Speaking about the experience in 2009, Mercer shared that one of their keys to survival was regular worship.[3] Each day, the group was allowed some time in the prison courtyard to get some fresh air—time that they leveraged to sing worship songs and pray. Heather later learned that the Taliban soldier guarding them was touched by their songs and overall resolve during captivity. After the Taliban's fall in Afghanistan, the prison guard traveled to Pakistan, sought out an evangelical pastor, and reportedly believed the gospel and was baptized. Though the group did not die as martyrs, they approached suffering with a posture of worship that enabled

1. See further Elliot, *Through Gates of Splendor*; Elliot, *Shadow of the Almighty: The Life and Testament of Jim Elliot*.

2. See further Liefield, *Unfolding Destinies: The Unfolding Story of the Auca Mission*.

3. Heather Mercer, Liberty University convocation, February 16, 2009.

them to endure the months in prison. They collectively witnessed through their worship as well.

Brother Yun (China)

The story of Chinese house church pastor Liu Zhenying, or "Brother Yun" (b. 1958), was captured in the 2001 book *The Heavenly Man*.[4] Following a dramatic conversion, Yun became an evangelist and a house-church leader in China. His ministry was characterized by visions, miracles, and hardship. Prior to receiving asylum in Germany in 1997, Yun was imprisoned in China numerous times in the 1980s and 1990s for preaching the gospel. Yun later joined Back to Jerusalem, a global missionary movement that pre-dated the Communist period. It focuses on mission to the least evangelized areas of the world between China and Jerusalem.

One distinct aspect of his ministry was responding to persecution and hardship with deliberate worship. As a house-church leader, he wrote new songs—often Scripture put to music—to encourage the underground church.[5] He reported:

> A deep revelation of God's love and presence flooded my being. I'd never enjoyed singing before but many new songs of worship flowed from my lips. They were words I had never learned before. Later I wrote them down. These songs are still sung in the Chinese house churches to this day.... When I first shared at Gao Village the Lord gave me Scripture songs to sing before the people. They wrote down the words so they could remember them.[6]

---

4. See further Yun and Hattaway, *The Heavenly Man*. Though some Chinese Christians have taken issue with some of Brother Yun's claims in the book, particularly his seventy-four-day fast, other Chinese believers have corroborated his ministry. See Hattaway, "An Open Letter Regarding 'The Heavenly Man,'" https://asiaharvest.org/open-letter-heavenly-man/ (accessed July 18, 2019).

5. See further Yun and Hattaway, *The Heavenly Man*, Kindle location 1853–91, 1915–25.

6. Yun and Hattaway, *The Heavenly Man*, Kindle location 410–501.

In Martyrdom We Worship

During times of hiding and fleeing from the Chinese authorities, Yun also worshiped. Describing one occasion of fleeing on foot, he wrote:

> Darkness had fallen in the mountains. I ran blindly through the hills and forests. I had no idea where I was heading, but just sought to put as much distance between the police station and myself as I could. As I ran I spoke out the Psalms with a thankful heart to the Lord, "Even in darkness light dawns for the upright, for the gracious and compassionate and righteous man. . . . Surely he will never be shaken; a righteous man will be remembered forever" (Ps 112:4, 6–8)."[7]

Yun also wrote and sang worship songs during periods of imprisonment. Through this, he remained encouraged. He wrote: "The more I sang the more I was filled with joy. I stood up and praised the Lord. Gradually my frozen hands and feet regained feeling and I wasn't cold anymore."[8] Yun also sang to the prison guards and his fellow prisoners. While this often irritated the guards, some prisoners embraced the gospel because of his singing witness. He also sang worship songs as a means of discipling and encouraging new believers in prison.[9]

Though Yun did not face martyrdom, his worship clearly demonstrates that he both expected and prepared for it. With one house-church group, he sang the following hymn:

> From the time the church was birthed on the day of Pentecost
> The followers of the Lord have willingly sacrificed themselves
> Tens of thousands have died that the gospel might prosper
> As such they have obtained the crown of life.
> To be a martyr for the Lord, to be a martyr for the Lord
> I am willing to die gloriously for the Lord.[10]

---

7. Yun and Hattaway, *The Heavenly Man,* Kindle location 710, 827.

8. Yun and Hattaway, *The Heavenly Man,* Kindle location 1095.

9. See further Yun and Hattaway, *The Heavenly Man,* Kindle location 1271, 1714–32, 1978–92, 2628.

10. Yun and Hattaway, *The Heavenly Man,* Kindle location 1001–7.

Christian Martyrdom

The Lord's Table in Somalia

Following a brutal civil war and famine that lasted from 1988 to 1992, Nik Ripken launched a network of humanitarian aid projects in Somalia. Ripken's organization provided food and medicine to some fifty thousand people a day. His staff consisted of Somali Muslims and Christians. Despite the good work the humanitarian group was doing, a radical Islamic group targeted the Christians and even some Muslims working with Ripken.

Despite the risks, Ripken and the threatened Somali believers continued their work. At one point, a small group of them met for worship—a prayer gathering and fellowship meal followed by the Eucharist. Ripken described the experience:

> Seven of us, three westerners and those four local believers, met at a pre-arranged time in the privacy of an abandoned, shelled-out building in the heart of Mogadishu—each of us coming alone from different directions. Once we had gathered and affectionately greeted one another, my friend led in a time of prayer and fellowship. We shared a light meal together. Then, as Jesus' followers have done for almost two thousand years, we shared the Lord's Supper in remembrance and celebration of Christ's willing and sacrificial death on the cross in our place, in atonement for our sins. We ate the bread in memory of His body, broken for us. . . . We drank the grape juice in remembrance of Christ's blood, shed for us. I wondered how many unnamed and unknown Somali believers had faced persecution, suffering, and death in this country for their faith. I felt honored to worship at the Lord's Table with these four brothers who were willing to risk their own blood, their own bodies, and their very lives to follow Jesus among an unbelieving people group in this unbelieving country. Never before had I felt the true cost and significance of Jesus' Last Supper with his disciples. This was a high and holy moment. It was also a moment that raised serious concern for our four believing brothers. The furtive and wary looks on the faces of my Somali friends served as a powerful reminder for me—a reminder not just of our Lord's death and sacrifice two

thousand years ago, but also a reminder of His continuing and constant love, His faithfulness, and His presence in the lives of brave and faithful followers today.[11]

Shortly after this worship gathering, the Islamists tracked down the Somali believers and murdered each of them. In their Lord's Supper worship, they remembered Christ's suffering before identifying with the Lord through their own martyrdom.

Coptic Martyrs

The Egyptian Coptic martyrs murdered by ISIS in 2015 exemplified worship amid suffering. Some of the men had been trained as choir members in Egypt. Since 100 percent of the Coptic liturgy is sung (as opposed to said), the choir assists the priest as worship leaders. These men would have been able to sing the entire liturgy by heart. With public worship opportunities limited in Libya, the men transformed their living space—one large room—into a worship area where they sang the liturgy, including prayers, hymns, and Scripture.

They continued to worship daily during their forty-three days in captivity before being beheaded. Each day, they were beaten and tortured and ordered to recite the *shahadah*, the declaration to become a Muslim. They refused. Afterward, the men collectively sang hymns and worshiped. One of the ISIS guards anonymously reported back to one man's family how impressed he was by their collective resolve to stand firm in their faith and worship while being beaten.[12]

---

11. Ripken, *The Insanity of God*, 115–16.
12. See further Mosebach, *The 21: A Journey into the Land of the Coptic Martyrs*, 122–30.

Martyrdom in the Church's Memory and Worship

Sacred Biographies

From the early church to medieval period, some eight thousand sacred biographies memorialize the lives of saints.[13] Though dismissed by some scholars as hagiography lacking historical value, the goal of these short biographies—including many martyr stories—was to teach faith through concrete examples. Through hearing and reading these accounts, believers have been encouraged to imitate the faith commitment of these saints and martyrs.[14]

Addressing the community of believers in Smyrna, the author of *Martyrdom of Polycarp* demonstrates this value. He writes: "we love the martyrs as the disciples and imitators of the Lord, and rightly so because of their unsurpassed loyalty towards their king and master. May we too share with them as fellow disciples!" He concludes that Polycarp "was not only a great teacher but a conspicuous martyr, whose testimony, following the gospel of Christ, everyone desires to imitate."[15] Similarly, the narrator of *Passion of Perpetua and Felicitas* opens his account asserting:

> The deeds recounted about the faith in ancient times were proof of God's favor and achieved the spiritual strengthening of men as well; and they were set forth in writing precisely that honor might be rendered to God and comfort to men; . . . should not then more recent examples be set down that contribute equally to both ends?[16]

During the Reformation period, the Anabaptist churches also published accounts of their martyrs. First published in 1660 in Holland, the *Martyrs' Mirror* became an inspiration to many Mennonite and Amish Christians. The *Chronicle of the Hutterite*

---

13. Heffernan, *Sacred Biography*, 12.

14. Smither, "To Emulate and Imitate," 146–52.

15. *Martyrdom of Polycarp*, 17, 19. Unless otherwise noted, all English translations of these are other acts are from Mursurillo, *Acts of the Christian Martyrs*.

16. *Passion of Perpetua and Felicitas*, 1.

Brethren captured the broader Anabaptist story from 1528 to 1665, which also included many accounts of martyrdom. The stated purpose of these works was "to preserve the memory of the myriad of martyrs of their faith and to connect them historically to the 'cloud of witnesses' recorded not only in biblical accounts but also in church history."[17]

From its origins, the Egyptian Coptic church has celebrated its martyrs. Even in the contemporary church, the Coptic liturgy includes readings from Scripture and the synaxarium—faith stories of saints and martyrs. Because of this, the Egyptian church experiences an integration of worship *(liturgia)* and martyrdom *(martyria)*.[18]

Feast Days

The church has also remembered martyrs by assigning them a feast day—a day on the church calendar that corresponds to the day of their martyrdom. Polycarp is remembered on February 23, Perpetua and Felicitas on March 7, Cyprian on September 14, and Latimer and Ridley on October 16. On these days, a portion of their biography is read while collects (short prayers) inspired by their faith and sacrifice are prayed.

Many church fathers also preached special sermons on these feast days, commemorating the testimonies of the martyrs and calling the church to imitate their faith. Among Augustine's hundred feast-day sermons for martyrs, he dedicated nine to Cyprian.[19] In *Sermon* 311, Augustine admonished the church to maintain the focus of a saint's day: "the right way to celebrate the festivals of the martyrs should be by imitating their virtues. It's easy enough to celebrate in honor of a martyr; the great thing is to imitate the

---

17. Butler, "'Church under the Cross': Anabaptist Theology of Martyrdom," 304.

18. See further Mosebach, *The 21: A Journey into the Land of the Coptic Martyrs*, 135–53.

19. See further Augustine, *Sermons*, 309–13, 313A-E; also Smither, "'To Emulate and Imitate,'" 153–55.

martyr's faith and patience."²⁰ Like authors of sacred biographies, Augustine's purpose in preaching about Cyprian and others was to encourage the church to imitate the martyrs' faith.

Buildings and Memorials

The church also commemorated martyrs by constructing church buildings on their burial sites. Following Cyprian's martyrdom in 258, a chapel was erected that was later expanded into a larger church facility. This was the space that Augustine visited with his mother prior to his conversion and departure to Italy. Later, as bishop of Hippo, Augustine preached a number of sermons in the Cyprian memorial church, including feast-day sermons honoring the martyred bishop.[21]

Venerable Bede (672–735), a historian of the English church, noted that a church structure was built in the early fourth century to remember St. Alban, the first English martyr (d. 305). Bede wrote: "when peaceful Christian times returned, a church of wonderful workmanship was built, a worthy memorial of his martyrdom."[22] Though at times these structures contributed to an unhealthy cult of martyrs, they also served as a visible reminder of faith to be emulated. St. Alban's Cathedral continues as an active congregation to the present day.

Shortly after their martyrdom in 2015, the twenty-one Coptic martyrs were canonized by the church. Through their faith, worship, and witness during suffering, they became a model for other Egyptian Coptic believers. In an unprecedented act, the Muslim government of Egypt funded a new church building in the martyrs' hometown to help the church remember their martyrs.

Sacred biographies, feast-day memorials and sermons, and even church buildings continue to remind the church of the faith stories of suffering and martyred Christians. These accounts

---

20. Augustine, *Sermon*, 311.1 (*WSA*).

21. See further Augustine, *Confessions*, 5.8.15; also Perler, *Les Voyages de Saint Augustin*, 440–76.

22. Bede, *Ecclesiastical History*, 1.7.

encourage other believers to stand firm in their faith in turbulent environments and even witness unto Christ through suffering. The memory of these martyrs—kept alive by the symbols of sacred biography, feast days, and church buildings—continues to stimulate worship today and helps the church to continually welcome suffering.

Summary

Worship is the beginning and end of Christian mission. John Piper famously asserted, "Missions exists because worship doesn't."[23] The purpose of making disciples among all peoples is that God would be worshiped and the unredeemed would become worshippers. Piper adds, "Worship . . . is the fuel and goal of missions."[24] Because we live in God's presence, tasting and seeing that the Lord is good (Ps 34:8), we are compelled by Christ's love (2 Cor 5:14–15) to share the good news with those apart from Christ.

In our short survey, we have seen that martyrs are worshippers. In many cases, these believers' worship practices (gathering for worship, preaching the gospel, or refusing to deny their faith) led to their martyrdom. When facing suffering and persecution, believers such as the Coptic martyrs or Somali Christians responded with deliberate worship. Finally, the martyrs' stories, captured in sacred biographies, feast-day sermons, and memorial churches, have inspired others to worship Christ. Suffering and martyrdom are acts of worship that have encouraged others to worship as well.

---

23. Piper, *Let the Nations be Glad*, 35.
24. Piper, *Let the Nations be Glad*, 35.

6

Reflections on Martyrdom for the Twenty-First-Century Church

Because we worship a Suffering Servant and because the Christian history has been marked by persecution and even martyrdom, suffering characterizes the Christian life. Given the claims that martyrdom leads to witness, prophetic voices, and worship, let us briefly reflect on what it means for the global church to be a martyr church in the twenty-first century.

First, the majority-world church must lead the way and teach the western church about dealing with suffering and martyrdom. By majority world, we mean the regions of Latin America, Africa, and Asia where the majority of the world's Christians reside. One hundred years ago, only 20 percent of the world's Christians lived outside of Europe or North America. Today, nearly 70 percent of the global church reside in the Global South. Though Latin America, Africa, and Asia have most of the world's Christians, pastors, and missionaries, they also experience the most Christian suffering.[1]

During the Iguassu Dialogue that met in Brazil in 1999, the assembled delegates, many of whom were majority-world Christian

---

1. See further Ripken, *The Insanity of God*, 145–322.

leaders, included this statement as part of their conference affirmation: "Suffering, persecution, and martyrdom are present realities for many Christians. We acknowledge that our obedience in mission involves suffering and recognize that the church is experiencing this."[2] This captures a perspective on Christian suffering held by many Chinese, Indian, and Middle Eastern Christian workers serving in their own contexts. It also sheds light on the experience of Christian missionaries *from* Brazil, Nigeria, and the Philippines laboring for the gospel in Muslim contexts like North Africa, the Middle East, and Central Asia. The majority-world church will continue to teach the global church about embracing suffering, resilience, and simple faith during persecution. Their testimony ought to convict the western church, which is often enamored with comfort, affluence, and a desire for political power.

Second, embracing suffering does not contradict the global church's commitment to labor for justice. The Iguassu delegates added: "We affirm our privilege and responsibility to pray for those undergoing persecution. We are called to share in their pain, do what we can to relieve their sufferings, and work for human rights and religious freedom."[3]

Over the last few decades, many western Christians, including elected officials, have advocated for suffering believers. They have appealed to leaders of nations that signed the 1948 United Nations Declaration of Human Rights, which includes article 18 on religion freedom:

> Everyone has the right to freedom of thought, conscience and religion; this right includes freedom to change his religion or belief, and freedom, either alone or in community with others and in public or private, to manifest his religion or belief in teaching, practice, worship and observance.[4]

---

2. "Iguassu Affirmation," 18.
3. "Iguassu Affirmation," 18.
4. "Universal Declaration of Human Rights." Online: https://www.un.org/en/universal-declaration-human-rights/ (accessed July 20, 2019).

Christian Martyrdom

Since the emergence of the Islamic State (ISIS) in 2006, the extremist group has worked to exterminate ancient Christian communities in Iraq and Syria. As a result, many Arab Christians have taken refuge in neighboring countries, including Jordan, Lebanon, and Turkey. Many international believers have raised awareness for persecuted Middle Eastern Christians by placing the Arabic letter nun (ن) on their social media accounts.[5] Some western Christian leaders and politicians have advocated for their resettlement as religious refugees in the United States and other western countries. Ironically, the United States government's increasing constraints on refugee resettlement since 2016, a move applauded by many evangelical Christians, has greatly limited the opportunity for persecuted Middle Eastern Christians to resettle in the United States.

In addition to these efforts in the political realm, others are laboring to train the next generation of global leaders to value religious freedom. Presently, an Iranian-American woman has launched a leadership network to train Middle Eastern women—leaders in politics, education, and business—to prioritize religious freedom as part of a vision for twenty-first-century human rights.[6]

Third, a biblical and historical reflection on martyrdom will help the church in the West to develop a greater capacity for suffering. By reading the stories of house-church leaders like Brother Yun in China or those interviewed by Nik Ripken in his work, *The Insanity of God*, western Christians have the opportunity to appreciate suffering and even gain a vision for it. As young American Christians consider a calling for global ministry, they will also embrace going to hard places for the sake of the gospel. They will strive to be faithful to God and to the Great Commission, placing that ahead of comfort, safety, or affluence.

Finally, this reflection on martyrdom should teach us that martyrdom is more of an attitude than an act. When the church father Origen of Alexandria (184–253) was eighteen years old, he watched his father die for his Christian faith. If it had not been

---

5. Nun represents the Arabic word for Christian, *nassarine*.

6. See further *Middle East Women's Leadership Network*. Online: http://www.mideastwomen.org (accessed July 20, 2019).

for his mother (who hid his clothes), Origen would have joined his father in martyrdom. Though he did not die that day (Origen died as an old man from wounds inflicted in prison during a later persecution), Origen understood that he was a member of a martyr church and this shaped his career as a teacher, theologian, and biblical commentator. Similarly, fourth-century church leaders Athanasius and Basil adopted a martyr's posture—a willingness to suffer and even die—as they stood up to political leaders and defended the purity of the gospel and sound doctrine. Similarly, during the late sixth-century mission to England, Bishop Gregory the Great asked Augustine of Canterbury and forty monks to embrace hardship as they traveled across Italy and France before preaching the gospel to the English. Though they wanted to turn back early in the mission, the bishop of Rome did not allow them that option.[7]

Many modern Christians have adopted an attitude that anticipates and welcomes hardship. After twenty-three years of pastoral ministry in Turkey, Andrew Brunson (b. 1968) was arrested and accused of crimes against the Turkish government. Brunson endured two difficult years in prison sustained by the support of his wife and a commitment to worship. Like Brother Yun, he wrote worship songs in prison.

In a more mundane, less dramatic form of suffering, a western couple spent almost three decades translating Scripture among a tribal people. Though they lived in a remote environment without electricity and had curses placed on them by a witchdoctor (who later believed the gospel), their greatest hardship came from other missionaries who criticized their approach to ministry. Yet, with a commitment to the Great Commission and an embrace of suffering, the couple endured and remained in their place of service until they believed their work was complete.

Most global Christians, even in parts of the world where Christianity is restricted, will not die for their faith. However, all Christians have the opportunity to imitate a Suffering Servant and welcome suffering, hardship, and pain. Christian martyrdom

---

7. See further Smither, *Missionary Monks*, 82–92.

teaches us to cultivate a theology and embrace of suffering as a normal part of the Christian life.

Bibliography

"The Apostles Creed." Online: http://anglicansonline.org/basics/apostles.html (accessed June 3, 2019).

Augustine. *Confessions. Sermons: Works of Saint Augustine: A Translation for the 21st Century*. Edited by John E. Rotelle, Volume III, Books 1–11. Hyde Park, NY: New City, 1994.

———. *Works of Saint Augustine: A Translation for the 21st Century*. Translated by Maria Boulding. Hyde Park, NY: New City, 1997.

Bede. *Ecclesiastical History of the English People; The Greater Chronicle; Bede's Letter to Egbert*. Translated by Judith McClure and Roger Collins. 1994. Reprint, Oxford: Oxford University Press, 2008.

Boersma, Hans. *Violence, Hospitality, and the Cross: Reappropriating the Atonement Tradition*. Grand Rapids: Baker Academic, 2004.

Butler, Rex D. "'Church under the Cross': Anabaptist Theology of Martyrdom." In *Celebrating the Legacy of the Reformation*, edited by Kevin L. King, Edward E. Hindson, and Benjamin K. Forrest, 299–316. Nashville: B&H Academic, 2019.

Claiborne, Shane, et al. *Common Prayer: A Liturgy for Ordinary Radicals*. Grand Rapids: Zondervan, 2010.

"Cranmer, Thomas." In *Oxford Dictionary of the Christian Church*, edited by F. L. Cross and E. A. Livingstone. Online: www.oxford-reference.com (accessed July 21, 2019).

Crosby, Cindy, ed. *Ancient Christian Devotional: Lectionary Cycle B*. Downers Grove, IL: IVP, 2011.

Cusato, Michael F. "Francis and the Franciscan Movement (1181/2–1226)." In *The Cambridge Companion to Saint Francis of Assisi*, edited by Michael J. P. Robson, 17–33. Cambridge: Cambridge University Press, 2012.

Daniel, E. Randolph. "Franciscan Missions." In *The Cambridge Companion to Saint Francis of Assisi*, edited by Michael J. P. Robson, 240–57. Cambridge: Cambridge University Press, 2012.

Davis, Leo Donald. *The First Seven Ecumenical Councils (327–787): Their History and Theology*. Collegeville, MN: Liturgical, 1988.

Bibliography

Dunn, Marilyn. *The Emergence of Monasticism: From the Desert Fathers to the Middle Ages.* Oxford: Blackwell, 2003.

Ehrman, Bart D. *After the New Testament: A Reader in Early Christianity.* New York: Oxford University Press, 1998.

Elliot, Elizabeth. *Shadow of the Almighty: The Life and Testament of Jim Elliot.* New York: HarperCollins, 2009.

———. *Through Gates of Splendor.* Carol Stream, IL: Tyndale, 1981.

Eusebius. *History of the Martyrs in Palestine, Nicene and Post Nicene Fathers* 2:1 http://www.ccel.org/ccel/schaff/npnf201.iii.xiv.i.html (accessed August 7, 2013).

Ferguson, Everett. "Martyr, Martyrdom." In *Encyclopedia of Early Christianity*, edited by Everett Ferguson, 724–28. London: Routledge, 1999.

Flemming, Dean. *Contextualization in the New Testament: Patterns for Theology and Mission.* Downers Grove: IVP Academic, 2005.

Fox, Robin Lane. *Pagans and Christians.* New York: Harper Collins, 1988.

Frend, W.H.C. *Martyrdom and Persecution in the Early Church.* Cambridge: Lutterworth, 2008.

Gallagher, Robert and Terry, John Mark. *Encountering the History of Missions: From the Early Church to Today.* Grand Rapids: Baker Academic, 2017.

Gesko, Gregory. "Early Monasticism and the Search for Friendship with God." Unpublished paper, Breck Conference on Monasticism and the Church, Nashotah House Theological Seminary, June 13–14, 2019.

Goehring, James E., "Monasticism." In *Encyclopedia of Early Christianity*, edited by Everett Ferguson, 769–775. London: Routledge, 1999.

Gregory of Nazianus, *Oration 43, Nicene and Post-Nicene Fathers* 2.7 http://www.ccel.org/ccel/schaff/npnf207.iii.xxvi.html (accessed October 4, 2019).

Harmless, William. *Desert Christians: An Introduction to the Literature of Early Monasticism.* Oxford: Oxford University Press, 2004.

Hattaway, Paul. "An Open Letter Regarding 'The Heavenly Man.'" Online: https://asiaharvest.org/open-letter-heavenly-man/ (accessed July 18, 2019).

Heffernan, Thomas J. *Sacred Biography: Saints and Their Biographers in the Middle Ages.* Oxford: Oxford University Press, 1992.

"Huss, John." In *Oxford Dictionary of the Christian Church*, edited by F. L. Cross and E. A. Livingstone. Online: www.oxford-reference.com (accessed July 21, 2019).

Hutton, J. E. *History of the Moravian Church.* London: Moravian, 1909.

"Iguassu Affirmation." In *Global Missiology for the 21st Century: The Iguassu Dialogue*, edited by in William D. Taylor, 15–21, Grand Rapids: Baker Academic, 2000.

Irvin, Dale T. and Scott W. Sunquist. *History of the World Christian Movement: Volume I, Earliest Christianity to 1453.* Maryknoll, NY: Orbis, 2004.

Jackson, Dave, and Neta Jackson. *On Fire for Christ: Stories of Anabaptist Martyrs.* Hatfield, PA: Herald, 1989.

Bibliography

"John Huss, 1369–1415, Pre-Reformation Reformer." https://www.christianitytoday.com/history/people/martyrs/john-huss.html (accessed July 20, 2019).

Justin Martyr. *First Apology*, Ante-Nicene Fathers 1 http://www.ccel.org/ccel/schaff/anf01.viii.ii.html (accessed April 13, 2012).

———. *Second Apology*, Ante-Nicene Fathers 1 http://www.ccel.org/ccel/schaff/anf01.viii.iii.i.html (accessed April 13, 2012).

Kalanztis, George. *Caesar and the Lamb: Early Christian Attitudes on War and Military Service*. Eugene, OR: Cascade, 2012.

King, Martin Luther. "I Have a Dream." Online: https://kinginstitute.stanford.edu/king-papers/documents/i-have-dream-address-delivered-march-washington-jobs-and-freedom (accessed July 12, 2019).

———. "I've Been to the Mountaintop: Online: https://www.cnn.com/2018/04/04/us/martin-luther-king-jr-mountaintop-speech-trnd/index.html (accessed July 12, 2019).

———. *Letters from a Birmingham Jail*. Online: https://www.africa.upenn.edu/Articles_Gen/Letter_Birmingham.html (accessed July 14, 2019).

"Latimer, Hugh." *Oxford Dictionary of the Christian Church*, edited by F. L. Cross and E. A. Livingstone. Online: www.oxford-reference.com (accessed July 21, 2019).

Liefield, Olive Fleming. *Unfolding Destinies: The Unfolding Story of the Auca Mission*. Grand Rapids: Discovery House, 1998.

"Malatya." Online: https://www.youtube.com/watch?v=4mSEeSZbejQ (accessed May 27, 2019).

Marshall, Paul. *Their Blood Cries Out*. Nashville: Thomas Nelson, 1997.

Marshall, Paul, Lela Gilbert, and Nina Shea. *Persecuted: The Global Assault on Christians*. Nashville: Thomas Nelson, 2013.

McDowell, Josh. *More Than a Carpenter*. Carol Stream, IL: Tyndale, 2009.

McMichael, Steven J. "Francis and the Encounter with the Sultan (1219)." In *The Cambridge Companion to Saint Francis of Assisi*, edited by Michael J. P. Robson, 127–42. Cambridge: Cambridge University Press, 2012.

Middle East Women's Leadership Network. Online: http://www.mideastwomen.org (accessed July 20, 2019).

Middleton, Paul. *Martyrdom: A Guide for the Perplexed*. London: T. & T. Clark, 2011.

Moorman, John. *A History of the Franciscan Order: From its Origins to the Year 1517*. Oxford: Clarenden, 1968.

Mosebach, Martin. *The 21: A Journey into the Land of Coptic Martyrs*. Walden, NY: Plough, 2019.

Moss, Candida. *Ancient Christian Martyrdom: Diverse Practices, Theologies, and Traditions*. New Haven: Yale University Press, 2012.

———. *The Myth of Persecution: How Early Christians Invented a Story of Martyrdom*. San Francisco: HarperOne, 2013.

Mursurillo, Herbert. *Acts of the Christian Martyrs*. Oxford: Oxford University Press, 1999.

Bibliography

Oden, Thomas C. *The African Memory of Mark: Reassessing Early Church Tradition*. Downers Grove, IL: IVP Academic, 2011.

Perler, Othmar. *Les Voyages de Saint Augustin*. Paris: Etudes Augustiniennes, 1969.

Peters, Greg. *The Monkhood of All Believers: The Monastic Foundation of Christian Spirituality*. Grand Rapids: Baker Academic, 2018.

Piper, John. *Let the Nations Be Glad: The Supremacy of God in Missions*. 1996. Reprint, Grand Rapids: Baker Academic, 2010.

"Ridley, Nicholas." *Oxford Dictionary of the Christian Church*, edited by F. L. Cross and E. A. Livingstone. Online: www.oxford-reference.com (accessed July 21, 2019).

Ripken, Nik. *The Insanity of God: A True Story of a Faith Resurrected*. Nashville: B&H, 2013.

Robson, Michael J. P. "The Writings of Francis." In *The Cambridge Companion to Saint Francis of Assisi*, edited by Michael J.P. Robson, 34–49. Cambridge: Cambridge University Press, 2012.

The Rule of Benedict: An Invitation to the Christian Life. Translated by Georg Holzherr and Mark Thamert. Collegeville, MN: Liturgical, 2016.

Schnabel, Eckhard. *Paul the Missionary: Realities, Strategies, and Methods*. Downers Grove: IVP Academic, 2008.

———. "The Persecution of Christians in the First Century." *Journal of the Evangelical Theological Society* 61:3 (September 2018), 525–547.

Short, William J., "The *Rule* and the Life of the Friars Minor." In *The Cambridge Companion to Saint Francis of Assisi*, edited by Michael J.P. Robson, 50–67. Cambridge: Cambridge University Press, 2012.

Showalter, Brandon, "Egypt's Copts Chant Nicene Creed After Palm Sunday Bombings," *Christian Post*. Online: https://www.christianpost.com/news/egypts-copts-chant-nicene-creed-after-palm-sunday-bombings-standing-strong-despite-massacre.html (accessed July 2, 2019).

Smither, Edward L. *Augustine as Mentor: A Model for Preparing Spiritual Leaders*. Nashville: B&H Academic, 2008.

———. *Missionary Monks: An Introduction to the History and Theology of Missionary Monasticism*. Eugene, OR: Cascade, 2016.

———. "'To Emulate and Imitate': Possidius' Life of Augustine as a Fifth-Century Discipleship Tool." *Southwestern Journal of Theology* 50.2 (2008) 146–66.

Stevenson, James. *The New Eusebius: Documents Illustrative of the Church to A.D. 337*. London: SPCK, 1957.

Sunquist, Scott W. *Understanding Christian Mission: Participation in Suffering and Glory*. Grand Rapids: Baker Academic, 2013.

Tertullian. *Apology, Ante-Nicene Fathers* 3. http://www.ccel.org/ccel/schaff/anf03.iv.iii.xxxvii.html, (accessed October 4, 2019).

———. *To Scapula, Ante-Nicene Fathers* 3. http://www.ccel.org/ccel/schaff/anf03.iv.vii.v.html (accessed April 13, 2012).

Bibliography

Tietz, Christiane. *Theologian of Resistance: The Life and Thoughts of Dietrich Bonhoeffer* Translated by Victoria J. Barnett. Minneapolis: Fortress, 2016.

Tucker, Ruth A. *From Jerusalem to Irian Jaya: A Biographical History of Christian Mission*. Grand Rapids: Zondervan, 2004.

"Universal Declaration of Human Rights." Online: https://www.un.org/en/universal-declaration-human-rights/ (accessed July 20, 2019).

Wilken, Robert L. *The First Thousand Years: A Global History of Christianity*. New Haven: Yale University Press, 2012.

Wright, Christopher J. H. *The Mission of God: Unlocking the Bible's Grand Narrative*. Downers Grove, IL: IVP Academic 2006.

Wright, James. *Martyrs of Malatya: Martyred for the Messiah in Turkey*. Welwyn Garden City, UK: Evangelical, 2015.

Brother Yun and Paul Hattaway. *The Heavenly Man: The Remarkable True Story of Christian Brother Yun*. Grand Rapids: Monarch, 2001.

Index

Anabaptists, 49–50, 64–65
Athanasius of Alexandria, 22, 37, 44–46, 71

Basil of Caesarea, 22–23, 45–46, 71
Bonhoeffer, Dietrich, 50–51, 56

China, xii, 60–61, 69–70
Constantine, Emperor, xiii, 18, 20–21, 44
Coptic Church (Egypt), 28, 40–41, 63, 65–67

Decius, Emperor, xiii, 19
Diocletian, Emperor, 20, 33, 37

Francis of Assisi, Franciscans, 25–27

Herod, King, 3, 7, 13

ISIS (Islamic State), 41, 63, 70

Jesus, xvi, 2–11, 15, 21–22, 26, 28, 30, 32–34, 40–42, 47, 51, 62
Justin Martyr, 32–35, 43, 56

King, Jr., Martin Luther, 52–54, 56

Latimer, Hugh, 48, 65
Monks, monasticism, 10, 21–26, 28, 45, 71
Moravians, 27–28, 47
Muslims, Islam, xi–xii, xv, 25–27, 40–41, 62–63, 66, 69–70

Paul, 3, 8, 10–15, 17, 21, 24, 57
Perpetua and Felicitas, 31, 36, 38–39, 44, 64–65
Polycarp of Smyrna, 18, 31, 39, 43, 64–65
Pontius Pilate, 7–8

Ridley, Nicholas, 48, 65
Roman Empire, xiii, xv, 10, 17, 20–21, 28, 33
Romero, Oscar, 55–56

Tertullian of Carthage, 34–36, 56
Turkey, xi, 70–71

Zinzendorf, Nicolaus Ludwig von, 27–28

www.ingramcontent.com/pod-product-compliance
Lightning Source LLC
Chambersburg PA
CBHW020212090426
42734CB00008B/1036